The Secret Life of a
MEADOW

The Secret Life of a
MEADOW

WILSON WALL AND DAVID MORGAN

WHITE OWL
AN IMPRINT OF PEN & SWORD BOOKS LTD.
YORKSHIRE – PHILADELPHIA

First published in Great Britain in 2023 by
White Owl
An imprint of
Pen & Sword Books Ltd
Yorkshire - Philadelphia

ISBN 978 1 39907 254 0

A CIP catalogue record for this book is available from the British Library.

Typeset in 11/14 pts Cormorant Infant
by SJmagic DESIGN SERVICES, India.

Printed and bound in India by Replika Press Pvt. Ltd.

Pen & Sword Books Ltd incorporates the imprints of Pen & Sword Books Archaeology, Atlas, Aviation, Battleground, Discovery, Family History, History, Maritime, Military, Naval, Politics, Railways, Select, Transport, True Crime, Fiction, Frontline Books, Leo Cooper, Praetorian Press, Seaforth Publishing, Wharncliffe and White Owl.

For a complete list of Pen & Sword titles please contact

PEN & SWORD BOOKS LIMITED
47 Church Street, Barnsley, South Yorkshire, S70 2AS, England
E-mail: enquiries@pen-and-sword.co.uk
Website: www.pen-and-sword.co.uk

or

PEN AND SWORD BOOKS
1950 Lawrence Rd, Havertown, PA 19083, USA
E-mail: Uspen-and-sword@casematepublishers.com
Website: www.penandswordbooks.com

MIX
Paper from
responsible sources
FSC® C016779

Contents

INTRODUCTION

Why we are writing the book and what a meadow is

Many people only have a vague understanding of what a meadow is and is not. This is not their fault; surprisingly few people have seen an established meadow and the confusion starts with the bulk of what is considered to be meadow actually being pasture. Meadows are different, as they are not routinely used as year-round grazing, while pasture often is. Pastures tend to be treated and over-grazed; meadows are untreated and gentle places that are easily damaged by excessive grazing.

There are many different types of meadow, depending upon the soil type and moisture content, each of which needs a slightly different approach. Water meadows, for example, have a high water table and often flood, mostly in the winter. On the other hand, meadows like my own that are on acid sand will dry out down to a depth of several inches in the summer. What does not limit a meadow is its size; they can be very small if managed properly, or on a scale that requires motorised machinery to cut them and can be used for winter grazing of livestock. Hay production is not seen as so important for agriculture now, but there is a growing understanding that for livestock, grazing on a meadow and eating proper hay makes for healthier animals.

Realising that meadows may be valuable to agriculture is a good thing, but it belies the sad statistics. Since the 1940s, 97% of flower-rich meadows across England have been lost, probably due to the necessary use of land for food production during the Second World War. This is a shame for many reasons, not least of which is something intangible that cannot be measured. A meadow is balm for the soul, and just to be able to sit and watch and listen is a wonder. The world contained in the meadow is getting on with its life, regardless of the machinations of man. One quiet county, tucked away from most visitors, has 20% of the remaining flower-rich meadows of England and that is Worcestershire. That there were so many meadows in this area originally is no surprise as they are frequently found in place names and boundary points. That they survived here more than anywhere else is less easily understood.

When that most august of documents, the Domesday Book, was produced in 1086, there were specific references to meadows. When these were added up by Oliver Rackham, he estimated that there were about 300,000 acres referred to, or about 121,000 hectares. This is only about 1.2% of the land, so they were obviously important. At the turn of the first millennium, it was recorded that not only were about 7% of meadows found in Lincolnshire, but the majority were in the East Midlands. Areas that were traditionally wooded tended to have less meadow, with exceptions. Around 1000 BCE meadows were very definitely rarer in the south-west of England than elsewhere, while pasture, which was routinely grazed and not kept for haymaking, was common in all counties. By the Middle Ages the amount of meadowland was increasing, and while it had been at a maximum level in Lincolnshire, the rest of the country had more or less caught up in terms of the percentage of land given over to meadows. It was around 1340 that this situation seems to have altered, and all due to the Black Death. Besides the personal horrors that such an epidemic wrought, the reduction in population as the disease ripped through the country meant that much arable land became meadow or pasture by default. Such was the indiscriminate nature of the disease that it sometimes involved changes in ownership as well, usually from the landlord to common ownership.

While these ebbs and flows in the fortunes of meadows were really just changes in the area that was turned over to grassland, it was in the seventeenth century that this situation changed. It was then that commercial seed production really got under way, changing the financial status of pasture and meadow. They could be ploughed and seeded, so by the middle of the nineteenth century meadows as we would think of them – flower-rich and with as many broad-leaved plants as grasses – were routinely ploughed and re-sown. To some extent this eased until the Second World War.

It was during the middle of the twentieth century that our exponential increase in population made it necessary for farmers to produce food on a much grander scale. The UK population in the 1930s was about 46 million and this was broadly fed from our farms. The increasing intensity of grassland agriculture has resulted in far more fodder grass being produced where large amounts of fertiliser is used. Unfortunately this has required several cuts a year, which start early. In fact they start so early that many species of wildflowers will be growing and possibly flowering, only to be cut down. This also affects the more delicate annual grasses as well as wildflowers. We ran a brief experiment on this many years ago to see whether residual seed in the ground would weather an inappropriate cut. We focused on yellow rattle (*Rhinanthus minor*), a species that is important in grass control. We only ran the experiment once because after we had cut the area with yellow rattle in flower, before seed production, it never came up again. A single badly timed cut can wipe it all out from an area. It is not unrealistic to think that other species are equally sensitive to such treatment.

The change towards silage production caused changes beyond reduction of plants species. Again, a simple example is that of the corncrake (*Crex crex*), which changed from a widespread species to one that by the 1990s could only be found breeding in Scotland, in the Hebrides and Orkney. Other species that have been hit, though not so hard, include the skylark (*Alauda arvensis*) and lapwing (*Vanellus vanellus*) these ground-nesting birds are disturbed in the middle of the breeding season. These birds, of course, need space, which requires a meadow of agricultural proportions. In a garden this is not possible, but the value to smaller creatures is just as large.

While it is a very easy process to turn an old and established meadow into an arable field, turning it back into a meadow is a rather more difficult process. Simply neglecting a ploughed field will result in a crop of the first wind-blown seeds to land. These are usually thistles, which can be difficult to control and, like bracken, invasive. The long-term result of neglected ground is for it to become heavily scrubbed and eventually wooded. The woodland may well not be as we would imagine it to be, the trees being widely scattered and surrounded by scrub. To stop this process and regain a meadow in a garden or field we need to understand that this is an ecology that needs maintenance, by human or animal intervention. This process of maintenance is significant as there are examples of changing the methods used to husband a meadow changing the character of the meadow. These changes can be as simple as moving from grazing being done by man, with a mower, to grazing by livestock. Even a change from one grazing animal species to another can alter the nature of a meadow.

Where small remnant areas of meadow flanks an area of the same land that used to be meadow, but has been turned to another agricultural form, turning the adjacent land back to meadow is not just a case of leaving the ground untouched. The plants that were wiped out from the change of use just do not return unaided. There will be an occasional attempt at invasion, but it is not a successful strategy for returning land to meadow. Always remember when you are setting up a meadow, whether garden or field, that the aim is to create an ecology that stabilises itself and this is an immensely complex process that will involve introducing species that will not find their way to your meadow unaided. For some species, introducing plants, or seeds, is the only way that they will ever arrive in your meadow. This is an obvious idea, but it has another side to it. Your meadow will not only provide shelter for all sorts of living things making up the tapestry of ecology, but your safe haven will be a stopping off point as well. It should not be underestimated just how important these patches and corridors of nature are in making sure that our world thrives.

There is an intrinsic understanding that meadows are beautiful places full of flowers, but suburban parks have shifted the perception away from reality and towards the idea that any green space without trees is a meadow. More recently an idea has arisen that has been wholeheartedly taken up by councils. This is that instead of having grass everywhere, why not spread meadow flower seed? This sounds like a good idea but these areas become high-maintenance flower beds and verges because the species that are planted tend to be transient annuals, which do not produce a long-term, stable meadow. The two primary and best examples of species like this are cornflower (*Centaurea cyanus*) and common poppy (*Papaver rhoeas*). Poppies especially will appear in huge numbers after many years of dormancy if a field is ploughed, allowing daylight to get to the seed in the ground. On bigger plots, this turnover of soil is carried out by moles and rabbits on a large scale, and by ants on a smaller scale.

While you, as the reader, may have sympathy for the idea of meadow creation and restitution, there is a group that we have to have some understanding for, even if we do not accept the result of their work – the farmers. During 2014 a protection plan was announced that would have given considerable protection to meadows. This was seen as an unacceptable intrusion by government into a farmer's use of land, with an unforeseen consequence according to a frequently quoted, but unpublished, report from Natural England. Immediately after the announcement, the rate of meadow destruction went up by a significant amount, the logic being that even though some of this grassland was well established and there were no plans for its reuse, if it was protected it could not be reused, so it would be better to plough it in advance to take it out of the equation. Not a good outcome for anyone, and certainly not for the meadow.

Tree planting schemes can also be to the detriment of ancient meadows. These meadows have often only survived to date because they are difficult to get at with farm machinery, being in awkward corners, on steep slopes or on a particularly infertile or boggy patch of land. Landowners provided with stewardship grants for tree planting will certainly be tempted to use their least profitable bits of land first. The ease with which this can happen was highlighted when the Woodland Trust, funded by Nestlé, started planting trees on a small, flower-rich meadow growing on a steep slope in Cumbria. When the Trust discovered what had happened the trees were removed, and the meadow restored.

How to use this book

Hopefully you will be as delighted as we are by the idea of producing a meadow and want to read this book through from the beginning to the end. But it should also hold you in good stead as a book for dipping into at various times to answer queries and questions that arise as you undertake your own meadow project. At the same time, you should not underestimate your own sense and ability to observe and witness the activities that carry on in your meadow and so make adjustments. A lot of our knowledge comes from doing just that and throughout the book we include the experience of creating our own meadows – a full-sized field that we refer to as the large meadow, and a converted back lawn in a suburban garden that we call the small meadow. In a well-tended garden you will probably know the names of all the plants that are present. In a meadow the number of species is immense, not just plants but animals as well. So although we illustrate and name many species, this book is not intended to be a definitive guide to what you will find; for that you need to use a field guide, such as the ones we list in the further reading section at the end of the book.

Our initial chapters in Part One describe the different types of meadows that can be found and their associated soils. This is a section worth reading as it will give you an idea of the type of meadow you can find in your area. More than that, it can give you a good idea of the sort of meadow that you can produce in your own garden or field.

Part Two is all about making a meadow. Not in a strict recipe fashion, but more in series of options and ideas that can be mixed and matched depending on your soils and your scale. The thinking behind this section is really that most people will be starting from scratch with their meadow projects. This can be quite a daunting prospect, especially with a garden project as it requires you to be prepared for unrestrained growth of grass and other plants in the first year.

In Part Three we will suggest some of the seasonal changes that can be expected in your meadow throughout the year. It is of interest that these will change, not just with the seasons, but as the meadow matures and different species wax and wane in number. The insects will also change through the seasons and through the years; sometimes certain species may be common, followed by years of scarcity. Bumblebee nests may come and go on an annual basis – this is quite natural, so long as the bees themselves still survive. Butterflies can also fluctuate wildly in numbers; marbled white butterflies (*Melanargia galathea*) were a common sight in our large meadow during 2019 but in 2020 we saw not a single one.

Although you may consider Part Four as rather academic, the ecology of a meadow is what makes it such a valuable resource for you and the planet. The future of meadows is also important; their protection and continuation as reserves of biodiversity is imperative if we are to continue to survive. The bumblebees that nest in our meadows will range far and wide to find pollen and nectar, and thereby provide pollination services for many of the plants that provide us with food, the fruit trees and bushes for example, since it is generally only cereal crops that are wind or self-pollinated. We should not underestimate the value of meadows; as reserves of plants and animals, from invertebrates to mammals, and as places that give respite from the more hard-edged aspects of life.

Throughout the book we will try and use common names for plants and animals that you may come across in your meadow. This may not always be possible as some species really do not have common names, and this is especially so with small invertebrate species and fungi that are rarely seen. We will, where possible, list the common names alongside the more precise biological names so that there is no confusion over which species are being described.

Part One

CHAPTER 1

A brief look at different types of meadow

The large meadow was a surprise to me. I had been to see it when the decision to buy was being weighed up by my good friends. It was early spring, the land had been used as horse pasture for years and was just green, like all of the surrounding paddocks and farmland. It seemed rather ordinary, notwithstanding the scrubby rocky outcrop halfway up its slope offering a rather tremendous view. What I had not appreciated was that this particular green was growing on rather thin, acidic, sandy soil. With the horses gone the slope became a mass of colour, mostly from annuals, totally different in character to the small meadow, which is on a neutral clayey loam.

Today's farmed grassland is so intensively managed that it tends to be green for the whole year and one's natural feeling is that it is all the same. Well, given the chance, it would not be. Take away the fertilisers and herbicides, the frequent ploughing and relaying and the multiple cuts or heavy grazing and soon wild flowers will appear among the grass. Which ones and how many depends on where you are, the new management regime and just how long you are prepared to wait.

It soon becomes clear when you do lots of wandering in the countryside that certain plants occur in certain places. Some are very obvious – bluebells in woods, bulrushes by water, buttercups in fields (Figure 1.1) – others less so perhaps because they are happiest with a certain combination of features or because they are less common. In fact, every species has its own set of needs.

There are three species of buttercup commonly to be found in meadows. They all have a fairly broad tolerance of soil conditions but each has its own preferences, particularly for soil moisture content. In order, from driest to wettest preference, they are bulbous buttercup (*Ranunculus bulbosus*), meadow buttercup (*Ranunculus acris*) and creeping buttercup (*Ranunculus repens*). Bulbous buttercup also has a bias towards more basic soils, while meadow buttercup likes ones that are a little more acidic. Because of the continuous variation in soil type and moisture content across the country, you can find meadows where just one of these species grows, others where

Figure 1.1. *As May progresses most meadows will be carpeted with bright yellow buttercups, in this case meadow buttercup, much to the joy of everyone wandering the footpaths through them.*

two grow together and a few where all three grow together. When they do all grow in the same meadow they will generally be separated into patches depending on soil chemistry and topography, which can be very subtle. For example, creeping buttercup will likely be in slight depressions where the soil is moister. If the field's farming history goes back to the medieval period and it still has the prominent ridges and furrows caused by the farming practised in those far-off days (shown in Figure 2.3), the buttercups will tend to organise themselves with bulbous on the drier ridge tops, meadow on the ridge sides and creeping in the damper furrow bottoms. No matter what the species composition, all of these meadows will be painted bright yellow in May when the buttercups are in peak flower. The small but significant changes in soil chemistry caused by the rolling topography of ridge and furrow meadows is sometimes picked out by other species as well. In springtime, Merry's Meadow in Rutland has cowslips (*Primula veris*) and green-winged orchids (*Anacamptis morio*) growing on the ridges and lady's smock (*Cardamine pratensis*) in the furrows. Even just a single species can highlight the ridges or furrows of ancient fieldworks (Figure 1.2).

Soil chemistry and moisture are not the only factors that affect plant growth, other aspects of the environment are important, too. Sometimes these will be necessary for the plant species to grow or flower, while in other situations it just means that a species is better able to tolerate them. Temperature is one such important factor – it gets colder as you go north or get higher and, on sloping ground, colder as you face north or east. Amount of light is another – there is less in shade and on a northern or eastern aspect. For both temperature and light, the joint effect of latitude and aspect is exaggerated as you move north because the sun is lower in the sky. The difference in the amount of light and the temperature between north- and south-facing meadows in Perthshire will be much greater than for the same meadows in Kent.

There are other 'buttercups', bright yellow members of the buttercup family, that show up in meadows but less commonly than the three we just met. They are more exacting in their needs and are good examples of a response to the other elements of the environment. Globeflower (*Trollius europaeus*) has a northern distribution and grows in meadows and pastures in hilly districts of Wales, the Pennines and Scottish Highlands, a variety of marsh marigold (*Caltha palustris*) can be found in wet upland meadows, while lesser celandine (*Ficaria verna*) will occasionally spread into meadows from the shade of adjacent woodland or hedgerows. If the meadow is so wet as to be boggy, lesser spearwort (*Ranunculus flammula*) may be the dominant buttercup.

Scientists have tried to quantify the influence of various elements of the physical environment on the growth of different plant species. They consider seven factors: soil pH, soil fertility, soil moisture, soil salt content, climate type, light availability

Figure 1.2. *Even a meadow full of the humble dandelion can look spectacular. The plants clearly prefer the better-drained ridges, demonstrating that even very small changes in topography can affect what grows in the meadow.*

and temperature. For every plant species they have given a score between 0, at one extreme, and 9, at the other, for each factor. This was done by measuring factor values at the sites where the species grow best. Since there are many other things that could be affecting the growth of a species, especially competition with other plants, these sets of values cannot be assumed to describe the optimum physical environment for the plant, they are just an indication, and are called the Ellenberg Indicator Values.

Other properties of the soil, such as structure and depth, are also important and some or all of these aspects may not directly affect the plant species but work via their effect on fungi. Very many plant species form associations with fungi, the fungi effectively mining the soil for nutrients that are passed onto the plants. The whole system is very complex, so a straightforward relationship between a physical factor and a species in a particular situation cannot always be shown.

You can find Ellenberg Indicator Values listed on the internet and they are quite helpful for meadow makers. First, you can find the values for a meadow by averaging the values for the species already growing in it. Even the values for an individual species growing in a potential meadow can be informative. If it is full of stinging nettle (*Urtica dioica*), for example, it will score a 9 for soil fertility and you will know that it is far too fertile to be able to create a species-rich traditional meadow. Secondly, you can do the reverse look-up. Knowing the values for a meadow, you can make a reasonable guess at the species that will prosper in it by looking for those whose values most closely match the field's values.

There are lots of species that could find a home in a meadow. We did a count through the *Flora of the British Isles* and found just over 380 described as native, or probably native, and inhabiting grassland, grassy places, turf or pasture. That is approximately a quarter of our native flora. Most of these, nearly 80%, are flowery forbs, what we call wildflowers in this book. They are the plants with the colourful flowers that are conjured into most people's minds when they think of meadows, the buttercups, cowslips, clovers, vetches, orchids, oxeye daisies (*Leucanthemum vulgare*), hogweeds (*Heracleum sphondylium*), sorrels and so on. We could add more wildflowers to our list if we included species that appear in meadows with unusual soil conditions. For example, high and very wet, bog asphodel *Narthecium ossifragum* or brackish, parsley water-dropwort *Oenanthe lachenalii*. Even so, many of the 300 wildflowers on our list are uncommon in meadows. Here are just a few examples: bird's-eye primrose (*Primula farinosa*) is only found on basic soils in northern England and southern Scotland; yellow-wort (*Blackstonia perfoliata*) has a southerly distribution and grows on calcareous soils; autumn gentian (*Gentianella amarella*) prefers the shorter turf of pastures with basic soils; mountain pansy (*Viola lutea*) grows in hilly districts perhaps with a leaning towards base-rich soils; common broomrape (*Orobanche minor*) is parasitic on clovers and common meadow species of the aster family and is restricted to England, becoming rarer to the north and west; round-headed rampion (*Phyteuma orbiculare*) grows on the chalk of southern England; sheep's-bit (*Jasione montana*) likes grassy places on sandy, lime-free soils; and meadow saffron (*Colchicum autumnale*) grows in damp meadows on soils that are not acid but it is quite rare and only found in England and south-east Ireland. Similarly, summer snowflake (*Leucojum aestivum*) is very local to the south of England and Ireland, especially in wet meadows along the Thames and Shannon. Whorled caraway (*Trocdaris verticillata*) is characteristic of damp, acid meadows in the west, and sulphur clover (*Trifolium ochroleucon*) grows on the boulder clay of eastern England.

Some others of our 300 wildflowers are more widely distributed but their typical habitats are not meadows. They have strayed into meadows because their characteristic habitat is adjacent to them. Several species that normally grow in shady habitats can be found in meadows with adjacent woods or hedgerows. It is quite common for lesser celandine, bluebell (*Hyacinthoides non-scripta*) and wood anemone (*Anemone nemorosa*) to do so. Similarly, lousewort (*Pedicularis sylvatica*), lesser spearwort and ragged-robin (*Silene flos-cuculi*) can creep in from areas of marsh and bog.

Figure 1.3. *A newly created meadow in Cumbria with many of the most ubiquitous meadow wildflowers – red clover, the white of oxeye daisy and the yellows of meadow buttercup and yellow rattle. Look closely and you can also see common mouse-ear and common sorrel.*

A handful of families provide many of the widespread meadow species (Figure 1.3). We have already described numerous buttercups, members of the eponymous family, the Ranunculaceae. They are, of course, the archetypal meadow plants. A close second are the clovers and vetches from the Fabaceae family. Their clusters of sweet pea-shaped flowers are magnets for long-tongued bumblebees and their roots, which are home for nitrogen-fixing bacteria, help to improve fertility in the meadow. Red clover (*Trifolium pratense*), white clover (*Trifolium repens*), common bird's-foot trefoil (*Lotus corniculatus*), tufted vetch (*Vicia cracca*) and hairy tare (*Ervilia hirsuta*) are commonly found in a wide variety of meadows. A third important group are the members of the broomrape family (Orobanchaceae). We will look in more detail later at these partial parasites on other plants in the meadow. Two are common in meadows: yellow rattle (*Rhinanthus minor*) and eyebright (*Euphrasia* agg.). There are a lot of species of eyebright and it takes an expert to distinguish between them, so most people treat them as a single aggregate group, hence 'agg.' in the scientific name. We meet two other sets of species later in the book that are equally difficult to identify and are mostly referred to using an aggregate name – dandelion, *Taraxacum* agg. and bramble, *Rubus fruticosus* agg.

The aster family, Asteraceae, are often called composites because their flowers are actually flower heads made from many individual flowers that have fused together. It is a very large family containing all of those yellow dandelion-like flowers, the white daisy-like flowers and the purple thistle-like flowers. Common yellow meadow plants are dandelion (*Taraxacum* agg.), cat's-ear (*Hypochaeris radicata*), autumn hawkbit (*Scorzoneroides autumnalis*) and goat's-beard (*Tragopogon pratensis*). The common meadow Asteraceae that are white are daisy (*Bellis perennis*), oxeye daisy (*Leucanthemum vulgare*) and yarrow (*Achillea millefolium*), and those that are purple are knapweeds. Another significant meadow family is the Orchidaceae, the orchids. We only have around fifty native orchids in the United Kingdom but almost three-fifths of them grow in grassland. The classic meadow orchid is the green-winged orchid. It has declined in parallel with the loss of traditional meadows, and now fields painted purple with green-winged orchids in the spring are mostly restricted to nature reserves. Common spotted orchid (*Dactylorhiza fuchsii*) is also a common denizen of traditional meadows. Another major meadow family is the Apiaceae, the celery family, those whose flower heads look like open umbrellas. Two are widespread in meadows: hogweed (*Heracleum sphondylium*), that giant of hedgerows, behaves itself in meadows, its flower heads raised just above the general sward, and pignut (*Conopodium majus*), which takes a long time to establish and its presence indicates a long undisturbed patch of ground.

Many more plant families contribute species to meadows, although not in the same numbers as those above. Three species from different families are perhaps the most ubiquitous: common sorrel (*Rumex acetosa*), from the dock family (Polygonaceae), is fairly inconspicuous in flower but then as the winged fruits expand and change colour the whole meadow can glow red. Common mouse-ear (*Cerastium fontanum*), from the pink family (Caryophyllaceae), is very common and quickly gets into newly created meadows, but its white flowers with deeply cut petals never have a big effect on the meadow panorama because the plants are too small and grow widely scattered. Devil's-bit scabious (*Succisa pratensis*), from the teasel family (Dipsacaceae), can turn a late summer hay meadow to a haze of blue, much like cornflower (*Centaurea cyanus*) used to do for arable fields, so long as the hay cut is timed fortuitously (Figure 1.4).

The other 20%, about seventy-five species, in our list of plants that inhabit grassy places are the true grasses and their allies, the grass-like sedges and rushes, which for ease of reference we lump together and call 'grasses' in this book. Although these are all green, close examination at flowering time reveals their beauty. A vase of meadow grasses alone makes a very attractive table decoration, and at one time they were sold for this purpose:

> Again there is work in the meadows – the haymaking is about, and the farmers are anxious for men. But the moucher passes by and looks for quaking grass, bunches of which have a ready sale.
>
> *The Amateur Poacher, Richard Jefferies, 1879*

It is a truism that grasses are fundamental to the meadow – meadows are a type of grassland after all. They are what the farmer was always striving to grow and they normally make up a big proportion of a crop of hay. A traditional meadow will have

Figure 1.4. *A glorious display of devil's-bit scabious in late summer thanks to a well-timed hay cut in the meadow of the old TB hospital nature reserve near Grassington, Yorkshire.*

a large number of grass species and, just like the wildflowers, the combination to be found in any meadow will depend on many factors. It is fair to say that for most people grass is grass, but go into a traditional meadow when the grasses are flowering and it is clear from the array of shapes and sizes that there are many species in the mix. The flower head of each genus tends to have a characteristic look that makes it relatively easy to tell, say, a fescue from a meadow-grass.

Like wildflowers, grasses each have their own set of preferences for soil conditions and other aspects of the physical environment, so some, having broad tolerances, are widespread, while others, with more precise requirements, have more restricted distributions. There are five true grasses in the family Poaceae that are particularly common in meadows. The first we should mention is sweet vernal grass (*Anthoxanthum odoratum*) because this is the plant that gives us the smell of new-mown hay. It has a rather untidy-looking, close-knit spike of flowers and starts to flower in April, hence vernal grass. Yorkshire fog (*Holcus lanatus*), named for its resemblance to the smoke billowing from northern factory chimneys when large quantities of it are in flower and viewed from a distance, is cosily soft to the touch and has a narrowly spreading spike of pinky-purple to white flowers. It is perhaps our most common and most widespread grass, and yet is not all that welcome in hay meadows because it makes poor-quality feed. Rough meadow-grass (*Poa trivialis*) is another very widespread species growing in all but extremely acid, dry or infertile soils. Although it rarely dominates the sward, it is present almost everywhere and we would venture to suggest that it is most people's idea of a typical grass. The small flowers are held in groups of two to four in an open, well-branched panicle. Although red fescue (*Festuca rubra*) can form dominant stands in some grassland situations, in species-rich meadows it usually appears as scattered individuals. Its rather large flowers, held in groups of four to seven, have bristle-like projections so that the narrowly open panicle looks rather coarse and shaggy. Finally, crested dog's-tail (*Cynosurus cristatus*) has a narrow and very neatly organised spike of flowers, looking a bit like a stack of miniature hair combs, atop a very thin, wiry stem. Since it is more resistant to heavy grazing than many others, it actually does better in pastures than meadows.

Most of the species in the other two families of grasses, sedges (family Cyperaceae) and rushes (family Juncaceae), are plants of wet conditions and only one of them is truly widespread and common in meadows. Although field wood-rush (*Luzula campestris*) is a quite a short plant, it starts to flower as early as March and its chestnut-brown flowers grouped into three to seven globe-shaped bunches stand tall above the rest of the sward, which is only slowly beginning to grow. You may know it without realising because it often grows in lawns. If you take a look at the leaves, they are quite characteristic of wood-rushes, being thinly covered with long white hairs.

Making up the final couple of places in our roll call of grassland plants are a couple of ferns: adder's-tongue (*Ophioglossum vulgatum*) and moonwort (*Botrychium lunaria*).

These are not like the big, leafy ferns with which we are all familiar. They are tiny, almost a hands-and-knees job to find, and they will never affect the overall look of a meadow. However, they are meadow specialists found only in unimproved fields that have been long undisturbed. Knowing that they are there lends a special aura to any meadow.

Imagine the variation there must be across the country in the physical factors described by the seven Ellenberg indicators and the number of possible combinations of them that are playing on the growth of our wild flowers. Add to this huge matrix of all the other factors that affect species in subtly different ways – latitude, altitude, aspect, soil structure, presence of soil fungi, root competition, shoot competition, time of germination, time of flowering, seed set and so on. The list is very long indeed and the upshot is that every meadow will be different because each plant species has its own likes and dislikes about each of the endless details of its environment. The combination of these together with the availability of seed of our 400 or so meadow plant species will determine the flowers that eventually grow in a meadow in any particular place. In this respect meadows are not wholly man-made. Humans play a part, of course, by their management of the land, but nature plays a significant part too and each meadow will tend to have its own character.

We will discover in Chapter 2 just how ubiquitous meadows used to be. The need for hay and the limitations of transport meant that at one time meadows were everywhere, across the whole country. As one moved around the country, the different types of meadow would have graded into one another. Today we are left with very few traditional hay meadows and the change in their character from place to place is no longer gradual. The regional differences are quite striking.

The most productive type of traditional meadow was to be found in the lowlands of England. These were the water meadows that used to blanket the flood plains of our big rivers. A few still exist, for example, along the Thames, Ouse, Avon and Deben. The most well-known is North Meadow at Cricklade (Figure 1.5). Its 44 hectares, that is roughly the size of sixty football pitches, has been managed for its hay crop in the same way for more than 800 years and this constancy has resulted in the gradual accumulation of over 250 species of wildflowers and grasses on the meadow and in the ditches that drain it. Between mid-April and early May the meadow becomes a stunning violet–purple haze when hundreds of thousands of snake's-head fritillary (*Fritillaria meleagris*) come into flower. This is when the meadow is at its most spectacular. The display of fritillaries is what it is famous for and justifiably so, because here you can see 80% of Britain's wild fritillaries. At this time of year there are fritillary guided walks and fritillary cream teas to be had in Cricklade. The meadow is hardly less spectacular once the fritillaries fade. By late April cowslips add a splash of yellow to the fritillaries, and then as spring turns to summer the meadow flowers ride the spectrum; purples of great burnet (*Sanguisorba officinalis*) and knapweed

Figure 1.5. *Massed snake's-head fritillary in North Meadow at Cricklade, Wiltshire; one of the few remaining water meadows in the country.*

(*Centaurea nigra*), brilliant yellows of meadow buttercup and yellow rattle, and whites of meadowsweet (*Filipendula ulmaria*) and oxeye daisy. Great burnet is one of the species typical of water meadows. The flowers attract a huge numbers of insects: twenty-three species of butterfly, nine of bumblebee and fourteen of dragonfly have been recorded in the meadow.

North Meadow is sandwiched between the Thames and the Churn. When these rivers flood the meadow, as they do every year at times between October and March, they are providing an essential ingredient to the meadow cycle by adding nutrient-rich silt to the neutral, alluvial soil. This winter flooding characterises water meadows and on many the flooding was managed with a system of sluice gates. Because these water meadows were so valuable, the common management style, as practised at North Meadow, was to divide the huge open areas into lots and to rent them out to local farmers so that each got their fair share. The allotment holders would cut the hay on their lot when it was ready, normally in early July, and they were required to have carted the hay by Lammas Day, 1 August. On that day the whole meadow was turned over to common land for grazing and commoners were allowed to continue grazing their livestock until Candlemas on 2 February, when the meadow was left untouched to grow the new season's hay crop.

Probably the most common type of traditional meadow was that growing away from river flood plains on the neutral, clayey soils that cover swathes of lowland England. We are lucky because a few excellent examples have been saved from the ravages of modern intensive farming. Eades Meadow, near Bromsgrove, is one such (Figure 1.6). Although it is the largest field in Foster's Green Meadows National Nature Reserve, the whole reserve is just 13 hectares in extent – you could fit three of them into North Meadow. Eades is exceedingly rich in wildflowers and grasses: over 180 species have been found in the meadow, on average forty are found in every square metre and in places the wildflowers predominate over the grasses. As with so many of this type of meadow, its flowering year starts in early May with one of Eades' stars, a spectacular display of massed, deep purple green-winged orchids. Later in the month cowslips and then buttercups turn the meadow yellow, before June brings a pink hue from a host of common spotted orchid. In June the wildflowers are at their peak and the orchids are joined by, among very many others, the yellows of yellow rattle, lady's bedstraw (*Galium verum*) and goat's-beard and the whites of pignut, pepper-saxifrage (*Silaum silaus*) and oxeye daisy. Still later in the summer, the purples return with common knapweed, betony (*Betonica officinalis*) and devil's-bit scabious. The flowering year is brought to a close in late August or September with Eades' other star, meadow saffron.

Eades is thought not to have been ploughed for more than 165 years and it has never been given artificial fertiliser or treated with pesticides. The management follows the traditional pattern practised on this meadow for 100 years or more. The year starts

Figure 1.6. *Once one of the most common types of meadow in the country, unimproved neutral grassland, meadows like Eades near Worcester often start the flowering year with big displays of purple green-veined orchids in early May (top) and then turn a subdued pink from massed common spotted orchid in June (bottom).*

and ends with the hay cut, these days in late summer, then over late autumn and early winter the aftermath is grazed by cattle and from late winter it is left alone to grow its hay.

Where the soil is a bit more basic on the boulder clay of the Midlands, the mix of wildflowers and grasses change to become closer to what you might see on chalk or limestone. The appearance of the grass upright brome (*Bromopsis erecta*) at Sudborough Green Lodge Meadow in Northamptonshire is taken to be an indicator of this, but the wildflowers show this, too. Salad burnet (*Poterium sanguisorba*), dwarf thistle (*Cirsium acaule*), fairy flax (*Linum catharticum*) and common milkwort (*Polygala vulgaris*) are all typical of calcareous soils. The rare sulphur clover also grows here.

In the northern Pennines and areas of southern Scotland another distinct type of meadow developed around a very characteristic farming pattern that possibly goes back to the time of the Vikings (Figure 1.7). The whole landscape has been moulded by hay and the harsh winter climate. In the valleys, small meadows, delineated by drystone walls, cluster around characteristic hay barns, situated well away from their farmhouses. The stone barns we see today probably started replacing timber barns in the early eighteenth century. Hay, stored in the upper storey, would be fed to cattle housed over winter on the lower floor, and the muck they produced was spread onto the meadows to fertilise next season's hay crop. In this way carting of the heavy hay and muck was kept to a minimum.

Over many centuries the practice of undisturbed hay growth on mostly neutral soils in the valley bottoms, although grading into more basic soils on the surrounding limestone hills, has allowed a unique caste of wildflowers to build up. These meadows are now mostly restricted to Swaledale, Langstrothdale and Wharfedale. Wood crane's-bill (*Geranium sylvaticum*) is characteristic and can be frequent enough to colour whole meadows, indeed they are sometimes called wood crane's-bill meadows. Also important are melancholy thistle (*Cirsium heterophyllum*) and globeflower and these are commonly joined by more widespread meadow species, meadow buttercup, eyebright and red clover. The precise composition depends on soil, slope and aspect. In Langstrothdale the neutral soils on the valley floor have more wood crane's-bill, common bistort (*Bistorta officinalis*) and common spotted orchid and the wetter slopes more great burnet, sneezewort (*Achillea ptarmica*) and globeflower.

As soils become wetter and more acidic towards the west of the country a more marginal type of meadow develops (Figure 1.8). It is generally known as Rhôs, which is its Welsh name. Other names are used locally elsewhere, such as Culm Grassland in Devon. Characteristically it is dominated by purple moor-grass (*Molinea caerulea*) and rushes, and where it is still managed traditionally, cutting for hay or litter in dry summers and grazing when the summers are wetter, it can become rich in wildflowers and grasses with as many as fifty species in every 4 sq m. Rhôs has its own mix of special wildflowers, like meadow thistle (*Cirsium dissectum*), devil's-bit scabious,

Figure 1.7. *The northern hay meadows of the Yorkshire Dales are characterised by field barns and two wildflowers, wood crane's-bill (bottom left) and melancholy thistle (bottom right). Indeed, they are sometimes called wood crane's-bill meadows. This one in Muker, Swaledale, has all but finished flowering by mid-July.*

globeflower and saw-wort (*Serratula tinctoria*), for instance, and in the wettest areas ragged robin, heath spotted orchid (*Dactylorhiza maculata*) and marsh violet (*Viola palustris*). Which ones are present in any particular meadow depends on its location and history. The meadow at Cae Bryntywarch near Trecastle in the Brecon Beacons, for instance, has bog asphodel and dyer's greenweed (*Genista tinctoria*). This sort of rough, wet grassland is very good for some of our declining wetland birds such as snipe (*Gallinago gallinago*), curlew (*Numenius arquata*) and reed bunting (*Emberiza schoeniclus*), and, where the right food plant is present, it is home to some special insects like the narrow-bordered bee hawkmoth (*Hemaris tityus*), which feeds on devil's-bit scabious, and the small pearl-bordered fritillary (*Boloria selene*) butterfly, one of whose food plants is the marsh violet.

As the soil conditions move further away from the generally moist, neutral clays or loams of the meadow types we have discussed so far, the land becomes ever more marginal for growing hay. Going higher and wetter than the wood crane's-bill meadows, as in many fields in Teesdale, the wildflowers are dominated by a recumbent form of marsh marigold. In lowland areas, where the ground water is basic, fen meadows can develop (Figure 1.9). Sweeney Fen in Shropshire is one such where water draining off surrounding limestone hills seeps into the peat. Here we have marsh marigold again, but the normal taller variant, and also bogbean (*Menyanthes trifoliata*), meadowsweet, wild angelica (*Angelica sylvestris*) and ragged robin, together with thousands of marsh fragrant orchids (*Gymnadenia densiflora*). Drier land on chalk

Figure 1.8. *Rhôs pasture at Killin, Scotland, in June, full of rushes and pignut.*

or limestone is sometimes used for meadows (Figure 1.10). The farm at Kingcombe in Dorset has pyramidal orchids (*Anacamptis pyramidalis*) and bee orchids in its chalky meadows, as well as species typical of this type of calcareous grassland, like common bird's-foot trefoil, rough hawkbit (*Leontodon hispidus*) and small scabious (*Scabiosa columbaria*). Dry acid soils tend towards heath. Harebell (*Campanula rotundifolia*) is a common plant in this habitat, together with a large proportion of clovers and vetches. Our large meadow is on such soil. Farmers would normally have used all these types of land for pasture, but no doubt there were times when such land was pressed into service as meadow, and each of the examples described here have been mown for hay.

With all of this largely predictable variation in the composition of meadow wildflowers and grasses you might be surprised to learn that there has never been a

Figure 1.9. *Fen meadow in early summer is very colourful, like this one, Sweeney Fen, near Oswestry in Shropshire. The overall impression (top) is just a froth of meadowsweet but closer inspection reveals marsh fragrant orchid (bottom left), marsh helleborine (bottom middle) and ragged robin (bottom right).*

classification system specifically for meadows. For farmers, the people who actually created them, they were simply a functional component of the farm, albeit an extremely important one. Farmers needed hay, so any land suited to growing it was turned into a meadow by the classic meadow-making management technique of a single hay cut, aftermath grazing, and, if necessary, annual application of manure and the occasional dusting with lime. Scientists – ecologists, botanists, conservationists – on the other hand have a system of classifying a habitat based on the community of plants growing there. This system, which describes all vegetation types from sand dunes to woodland to mires, is called the National Vegetation Classification. Each vegetation type has a code (like MC for Maritime Cliff Communities) and each community within that type is given a number and a name, which is a couplet of the names of two plant species always found in that community. There are three grassland vegetation types describing communities growing on acid through to basic soils – U for calcifugous grasslands and montane communities (acid), MG for mesotrophic grasslands (neutral) and CG for calcicolous grasslands (basic) – and each of these has about a dozen grassland communities, many of which are divided once again into sub-communities. Meadow is not a vegetation type in the NVC scheme. Meadows could be made from any of the grassland communities, although very many of the old meadows were from only a few communities, perhaps the most common being MG5 (crested dog's-tail common knapweed), which is unimproved neutral grassland, and MG4 (meadow foxtail great burnet), which is seasonally flooded, unimproved, neutral grassland. The problem of trying to use the scheme to describe a meadow is that sometimes it will be on a boundary and cannot be assigned to a community, and sometimes it will contain more than one community. What is more, the NVC tells us what a patch of ground is now, not what it was or what it could be, which is mostly what we are interested in in this book.

Of course, wild flowers and grasses are not the only things living in a meadow. Animal distribution is affected by the same environmental factors as plants and, generally speaking, the smaller the animal the more this holds true, in part because smaller animals are more likely to be dependent on specific plants. So can meadow types be defined by the animals found in them just as they can by the plants growing in them? Not so much. The meadow will only be a small fraction of the territory of large mammals – such as deer, fox (*Vulpes vulpes*) and badger (*Meles meles*) – while smaller animals like mice and insects that actually live in the meadow are at great risk from the hay cut. Thus, whereas the meadow management is key to making a home for the mix of plant species found there, it destroys the home of smaller animals. That is not to say that meadows are unimportant for smaller mammals, insects, spiders, snails, and other invertebrates, because they are. Their importance comes more from their part in the mosaic of habitats surrounding them – woodland, hedgerows, verges, marshes, streams and riversides etc. The meadows provide a bountiful source

Figure 1.10. *Taller calcareous grassland is sometimes cut for hay. In the mix in this one is pyramidal orchid, lady's mantle, bulbous buttercup, red and white clover, common bird's-foot trefoil and rough hawkbit.*

of food, especially during the spring and early summer and even in the autumn and winter from late-flowering wildflowers and the dung of the aftermath grazers. Having said this, there are small animals that specialise in the various grassland types and sympathetic management of the meadow community can encourage these, like those narrow-bordered bee hawkmoths relying on devil's-bit scabious in Rhôs.

Fungi live in meadows as well, for the most part hidden underground, and, since many of them only grow into toadstools irregularly it can take many years to discover just how many species there are growing in a meadow. The classic meadow fungi are the waxcaps, a colourful group that includes the true waxcaps plus earth-tongues, pinkgills and fairy clubs. In traditional, undisturbed meadows this group can account for 40 to 70% of the total fungal biomass. They tend to be found in wetter, though not waterlogged, meadows growing on soils the acid side of neutral. Often the best waxcap meadows are the poorest for wildflowers and grasses. In water meadows on better soils, mushrooms, like field mushroom (*Agaricus campestris*) and horse mushroom (*Agaricus arvensis*), are more typical.

Even though they are hidden, fungi, just like the small animals, are important for the health of the meadow.

CHAPTER 2

The importance of meadows to agriculture past and present

Agriculture, in the sense of planting a crop as a monoculture, has a long history, but this is probably pre-dated by grazing animals under domestication. Grazing would have been controlled once a village became an established settlement and the farming community was no longer a travelling group. The development of meadows naturally followed on from this to provide winter fodder and bedding for livestock. Unless a meadow is large, routine grazing throughout the seasons can be quite detrimental to the flora and fauna. This in turn will result in degraded food stocks for the grazing animal, especially if the animals congregate in one corner of the field.

It may seem counter-intuitive, but sadly for modern agriculture the meadow has little to offer. The reason is that in the rush to provide food for a burgeoning population and make a living, the production of food has become a business, and only a business. So in the same way that for most people handmade clothes are an unlikely purchase, so food from a traditional method of agriculture is also an unlikely find. We do not mean just the produce labelled as 'organic', which conforms to an arbitrarily constructed set of modern standards, but those grown in a garden or allotment that has neither weedkiller nor insecticide applied. Growing food in this way is so labour intensive that the end product would be prohibitively expensive. This, sadly, means that for the modern commercial agrarian, the meadow has no place in the scheme of things. All fields have to pay their way, which without subsidies meadows do not. Food production has become a measure of chemical input and saleable food output. One of the important components of a meadow is as a reservoir of pollinators that need flowers to feed. Now, for crops such as cereals, this has no significance as these are all either wind pollinated or self-pollinated. Other crops that are simply dependent on air and water to produce a crop, such as root and leaf vegetables, also don't need pollinators, but for other crops this is not the complete story.

For any crop that requires insect pollinators, the story is quite different. A high-input farming system will have several detrimental results. The primary one is a reduction in pollinating insects. For nearly a century the reduction of pollinators on farm land has not been noticed, even though it has been significant. The first obvious change that would be seen is a drop in crop production, so why was this not spotted earlier? The answer lies in the verges and marginal hedges that have been acting as reservoirs for pollinating insects in lieu of meadows. Without these areas crop production would have been reduced. The farm is despoiling the bulk of the land and yet still relies upon the areas outside their jurisdiction for pollinators.

For modern farmers, then, we can say that they are dependent on meadow species, but not on meadows. This makes any meadow that still exists very much an area that is of inestimable value to wildlife, but by modern accounting standards, of no monetary value to the farmer. Unless you have had the pleasure of sitting in a meadow you may never have felt the calmness that such a place can engender (Figure 2.1). So we can change our statement about the value to wildlife to a meadow being of inestimable value to wildlife and humans alike.

In past centuries, meadows were essential to the farming community to provide fodder and bedding during the cold and wet seasons. Because the biodiversity of the times was at a peak throughout the countryside, the need for meadows as reservoirs of pollinators was not as essential as it is now. The state of the hay that was made from

Figure 2.1. *A traditional meadow near Bromsgrove, well-known for its orchids.*

traditional meadows was extremely good as the variety of fodder that was available constituted a complete diet for the livestock when grazing was not possible.

On modern grass-based pasture, roots tend to be shallow, so all of the trace elements that appear in the grass come exclusively from the very top of the soil. There is also the consequence of monoculture grasses not being able to extract all of the rarer elements that are necessary for healthy animals. If this is compared to a well-mixed meadow, where grass is often a minor component, or at least not a dominant one, the bulk of the species are dicotyledon plants, rather than the monocotyledon grass. These tend to have much more robust roots, often long and deep. Roots such as these can mobilise mineral nutrients from deep in the soil, much of which will be returned to the surface layers after the plants die in the autumn. If cut and used as hay, these nutrients find their way into the livestock food chain, improving both animal health and growth. Modern agricultural practices have moved away from this, towards feed supplements instead, while still maintaining a heavy dependency on monoculture grass animal feed.

In a traditional system, once the meadow had been cut – once or sometimes twice, depending on the soil type – the meadow would have been used as winter grazing. Here again, there is a large gap between the techniques of grazing found in mediaeval meadow culture and modern pasture. The most significant difference is the animal load per acre. In times past the number of animals in a field was directly related to the size of the field. In the second half of the twentieth century artificial feed made it possible to overstock fields as a routine, which has resulted in over-grazing reducing the range and size of plants growing in the sward.

In more recent times, grazing rates have been calculated based on a commercial level at which over-grazing is avoided. This has been carried out using either Livestock Units (LU), where the cow is 1LU or a modification of this system. Around 2006 the Livestock Unit was modified so that the grazing load was based on the mass of the animal divided by 650. It was all intended to maximise output without causing over-grazing and poaching of the ground caused by excessive hoof damage. However, such calculations are intrinsically flawed for two main reasons. The first is trivial in that while cows happily graze long grasses, horses preferentially graze short sward areas, even to the point of over-grazing some areas rather than moving into long grasses. The second is more important as it reflects our disconnection from the biology of our world. All such calculations are based on what we, humans, can get from the land. It takes no notice of the land and its plants and animals for their own sake. The energy flow is calculated in one direction only and as such cannot have a good long-term outcome for the planet.

If we look backwards to a time of lower inputs and lower outputs, a different story is found. It is in older systems of agriculture that the value and legacy of meadows is to be found. It is also here that we find the reason that we should all start developing our own biodiversity projects. As a steady form of land use, meadows were the most common description that was referred to in the Domesday Book of 1086. The reason for this is simple as it was land often held in common, and it maintained the health of the livestock of the village. The meadow was a mainstay of the traditional three-field system that was in wide usage until it began to be phased out during the seventeenth century. This form of agriculture was of a significance beyond its own span; it not only lingers on in the allotment system but can still be seen in the undulating landscape of parts of Britain.

Large communal fields would have been laid out in strips using field markers, which eventually become recognisable in the landscape as ridge and furrow fields. This visual affect was due to the practice of ploughing from the middle and turning the plough at the end of the furrow always in the same direction so that the plough alternates from one side of the strip to the other, gradually working from centre outwards, almost in spiral fashion. This gradually results in a small accumulation of material in the centre, and after many years a ridge can be seen in the centre and the edge becomes the furrow (Figure 2.2). The strips of land tended to be a furlong in length, but of variable width, resulting in a field that varied from a quarter to an acre in area (Figure 2.3). It is interesting that the alliterative poem 'Piers Plowman', written between 1370 and 1390, has a section where he cajoles helpers to assist in ploughing his field of half an acre, presumably part of a ridge and furrow system. This ploughing regime was carried out using oxen, which would have been fed on the communal meadow over winter and received a great deal of fodder from it at other times of the year, as well as from the fallow field. As they were feeding in one area and working

Figure 2.2. *The method of ploughing that gave rise to the ridge and furrow field. The ploughs were single-sided, turning soil to the right, so ploughing was done in a clockwise direction. This would start in the middle, plough up the line, turn right and return down line two, then turn right and the next plough line would be number three. This threw up the soil in the same direction every year, eventually moving the soil to form the ridge and furrow appearance.*

Figure 2.3. *Telltale signs of ridge and furrow ploughing from past centuries in a contemporary grazed field at Childswickham in Worcestershire.*

in another, there was an automatic transfer of natural fertiliser from one part of the system to another.

During this period of history, there was an interesting aspect to the health and well-being of the population that is sometimes lost amid stories of Black Death and serfdom. Measurement of skeletons from the Middle Ages shows that they were taller than their Roman forebears, although the story needs to be looked at in more detail as there is more to this than that simple statement contains. All of these calculations of height were made based on excavated skeletons, so although any given one might not be accurate, the overall statistical picture is.

During the Roman occupation, in about 200–410 CE, height increased from 167cm to 170cm. This is thought to be directly attributable to a better water supply and better sanitation. This increase seems to have been maintained until around the year 600, when it started to decrease with the slow decay of the Roman systems for delivering water and removing waste. After this period there were several measured fluctuations in general height associated with a reduction in the rural population and a period of lower than average summer temperatures. The plague years of 1348–1350 marked a change in fortunes for the population of the UK, with an increase in agricultural production and fewer people to feed. This better diet was responsible for a period, from 1400 to 1700, when the average height was about the same as it was during the twentieth century. The decline since the eighteenth century matches the rise of the industrial revolution, while the increase during the twentieth century matches the rise of high-input agriculture and better public health.

During the time when meadows were an integral part of farming, necessary to keep the land healthy and productive, the methods used to tend the meadows were beneficial to wildlife as well. It was quite normal practice for the hay cutters, who would have been using hand tools, scythes and sickles, to spot the nests of ground-nesting birds and work their way around them. These small islands would become havens in which fledglings could find shelter from predators without fear of damage. Introduction of mechanical cutters, initially horse-drawn, made this much more difficult to accomplish, so within one generation the lore associated with this process of haymaking was lost. A direct consequence of this was a steady decline in birds such as corncrakes (*Crex crex*), skylarks (*Alauda arvensis*) and other ground-nesting birds, as well as the brown hare (*Lepus europaeus*). During the nineteenth century, corncrakes were said to nest across the whole of the UK, but by the time of a bird census in 1993, there were only 480 birds found, mostly in the Hebrides. Allied to this blanket cutting was the growth in the automated timing of cuts, which were often carried out when other activity on the farm was at a low ebb. This would often result in cutting far too early, taking off the flowers of plants instead of letting them set seed first. This can be done occasionally to perennial species without too much harm, but annual plants that do not have a reservoir of seed can be wiped out by a single inappropriate cut. One of the pivotal meadow species, yellow rattle (*Rhinanthus minor*), is a very good example of this and is also an example of a plant that is central to the diversity of a flower meadow. Important aspects of this species are described in Chapters 4 and 5.

At the same time as mechanised pasture cutting was developing, there was another change in practice that also caused a major alteration in flora and fauna of parts of the UK. It had been the practice in upland parts of the UK to rear sheep during the winter in the lowland areas where they could be fed and tended and then, in late spring and summer, to take the flock into the hills. These high meadows would then be grazed throughout the seasons until it was time for the flock to move into winter quarters in the valley. This rotation of grazing mirrored the arable practice of leaving a field fallow. The land was never exhausted and the inputs and outputs were broadly balanced. In some parts of Europe these seasonal meadows are still very much part of the agricultural scenery, but elsewhere they have disappeared. Flocks tend to have year-round pasture with additional food being taken to the animals when the weather precludes natural grazing. By constantly grazing the same area, the species mix of plants is reduced and the resilient species become dominant and take over. This has been described as the method by which some of the most denuded green desert pastures in the modern world have been created, second only to the monoculture found in large-scale arable fields. The problem is not just a reduction of flowering species, bad enough in itself, but the knock-on effect of a reduction in insects and other invertebrates, which means a reduction in the insectivorous birds and animals and those species that live on them. This is a loss of biodiversity, which we can help to rectify by making our own meadows.

The mechanisation of farming practices is a major contributor to this situation. It is undoubtedly easier to cut a pasture for silage when the grass is ready than to wait while flowers seed, but this rapidly depletes the land of everything but grasses. This denudation is not just of wild flowers but the birds, mammals and insects that go with them. Even species of butterfly that are associated with grassland, such as marbled white (*Melanargia galathea*), need a specific habitat, with time for them to live and breed on long grasses.

Such is the change in agricultural practices that many species have been pushed to the margins, where, over the last seventy years of published field guides, the picture drawn is one of reflecting reality rather than possibility. By pushing species such as the marbled white butterfly into low-productivity areas that still retain suitable species they become associated more with the terrain than the distribution of the flora. In the case of the marbled white butterfly, it is routinely described as a species of chalk hills, but it has a very healthy population living on our lowland acid meadow, which has the right food plants, red fescue (*Festuca rubra*) and Yorkshire fog (*Holcus lanatus*). This in some way reflects the developing gap between where plants and animals are found and where they were found. The historic range of species, both plant and animal, is key to understanding something very important about the landscape. It is only in more recent times, the last 150 years, that the landscape has become what appears to be a series of different small areas of cultivation. Before this time they would have all been joined and surrounded by corridors and patches of meadow-like growth. This integrated system of cultivation would have enabled gene flow between different populations of plants and animals.

Until the twentieth century, what would have been a contiguous system of plants and animals across large stretches of the landscape could effectively be seen as a single population. There would, of course, have been natural barriers, such as large rivers, but in general terms the populations were large and extensive, rather than small and fragmented. This was important for gene flow to stop small natural populations becoming isolated and inbred. When small isolated populations have a severe dip in numbers, they may recover, but with a reduced genetic diversity, or with an altered and skewed genome. This lack of genetic diversity can result in what is in effect an inbred population susceptible to disease. It was the changes in agricultural practices taking place in the middle of the twentieth century that were going to put considerable strain on maintaining genetic diversity in wild populations. These small populations are also susceptible to single events, such as flood or drought, completely wiping them out.

From the 1930s onwards, chemical fertilisers became more commonly used, which favoured some of the most vigorous species to the detriment of less vigorous species, which would then be pushed out of the pasture. Such an application of fertiliser would change the composition of a meadow after a single application by reducing the biodiversity. It was the use of fertilisers and weedkillers, in conjunction with a looming food shortage, that really hit meadows hard, with them taking the brunt of a wider onslaught on our landscape. After the vicissitudes of the Second World War there was a desire for change of all sorts and much to the surprise of the political establishment, the General Election of 1945 saw Winston Churchill defeated and a Labour government under Clement Attlee swept to power. This was going to be a period of change in many aspects of life, not least agriculture. In 1947 the government introduced the Agricultural Act, in part at least, as an attempt to regain food independence. Food shortages were still commonplace at this time, so any attempt to increase food production was seen as a good thing. As a policy this was an extension of the process that had been going on throughout the war. The sad part of the process was that there was no flexibility in the system and when the man from the Ministry of Agriculture came knocking, the land you thought was your own became liable to a change of use, whether you liked it or not. This very often involved ploughing land that had previously been used as pasture, and of meadows. As these changes of use included some very old and established meadows, the damage would not be easily ameliorated, even if the will to do so was there, which very often it was not.

The 1947 Agricultural Act codified the power of the Ministry of Agriculture. Although this legislation is usually considered to have been motivated by getting Britain feeding itself, the reasoning behind the legislation was a little more contentious. The government wanted to have a better balance of payments and a way to do this was through agriculture growing exportable produce. So by 1951, domestic agriculture was worth about £100 million annually, of which about half was exported. Of course, meadows have nothing to export and so come far down the list on any commercial scale. This, in broad terms is why about 95% of meadows have been lost in the last seventy years, not even a lifetime. It would seem that some parts of the country were too far for the men from the ministry to visit regularly, so 20% of the remaining meadows can be found in one county, Worcestershire.

Regularly re-sown leys of pure, vigorous fodder varieties that are cut young for silage mean that green fields are now often monocultures of perennial rye-grass (*Lolium perenne*) and almost insect free. This is not helped by the trend in dairy farming for keeping herds indoors, fed on silage. There are fewer cowpats in fields for fly and beetle larvae to feed on, and, in fact, those that are there are often toxic to insects because of drug residues they contain from veterinary treatments. Loss of insects from meadows is a big contributor to the reported 70% decline over twenty-six years found in flying insects that was reported in a German study.

Creating or restoring meadows is a time-consuming activity. It really is not difficult, as we shall describe later, but to gain the richness and balance that a traditionally managed meadow has, does take time. In many ways it is unreasonable for farmers to give up land for an intangible benefit, which sadly can be misused. For modern walkers in the countryside the understanding of a meadow seems to have been lost, and tramping across them seems to be acceptable behaviour. It is almost as if they represent nothing more than a big lawn grown for their benefit. What we should recognise is that the presence of meadows indicates a healthy landscape of great diversity. Contrary to their image portrayed in the twentieth century as reservoirs of weeds, they are seen more and more as reservoirs of biodiversity, pollinators and predatory species that will help control crop pests. Unfortunately, while hedges and meadows are being restored in some areas, it is not universally so. One of the apparent results of this continued decline in the fortunes of the natural landscape is a reduction in the numbers of butterflies, reportedly by 50% since 1975 in the UK. That such trends continue in a downwards direction reflects the need for all of us to try and create our own meadows, whatever the size.

Once a meadow has been ploughed up and starts producing a profitable crop, it is very difficult for a farmer to justify returning it to a condition that has little or no financial value. Even with subsidised systems this has been difficult, because a meadow is not neglected land. It needs to be managed as much as any arable crop to be able to thrive. As we shall see, there are costs involved in looking after a large meadow. There are even more when it is returning a field used for arable crops to meadow. Possibly the least expensive transition is from dairy or sheep pasture to meadow, but even here it takes more than just neglect and removal of unseasonal grazing animals to return a field to a meadow. All of these changes require some financial input and a lot of goodwill on the part of the landowner; very often the return of farmland to meadow is seen as producing an 'amenity'. This is quite the wrong the way to look at such a change.

Moving from a commercial farming cycle to the financial liability of a meadow should be looked at in a quite different manner to the way farming has been dealt with for the last century. We should start by appraising our attitude to where we live. As a concept 'the land' is not a disposable product to be used as we want, it really does need to be looked after. If we do not, there could be unknown repercussions that can come back and bite us. When a meadow is created, or restored, there is more going on than simply a change in biodiversity. The process is long, and it says something about the creator of the meadow. It says that you care about the land and its future. There is more to this than the simple idea of keeping a plot for the benefit of future generations. Thinking in those terms is wrong; it implies the meadow is a commodity, which, of course, it is not. It is a complex environment, a super-organism, if you like. Setting up or restoring a meadow is something of which you can be proud; it shows a belief in the long-term survival of your plot. It is not just another transitory crop, it is one of the few uses for land that is enhanced by long-lived plants, which need time to grow and develop. Some of the plants that you see in a meadow may well have been there for more than twenty years. These long-lived meadow plants are often forgotten; it is not just trees that have long lives spanning decades.

The enormous diversity of plants, animals and fungi that survive and thrive in an established meadow will undoubtedly help in the survival of pollinators. These may well help with the pollination of surrounding crops if they need an insect pollinator. If it is in your garden, you may be pleasantly surprised by an increase in fruit from your trees and bushes aided and abetted by bumblebees living in what was your lawn but is now your meadow. In our meadow we regularly have carder bee nests, although they tend to move around and vary in number from year to year. Besides being general pollinators, and lovely insects to have around, these bees are extremely good at pollinating clovers that honey bees do not have the tongue for (Figure 2.4).

Bees are not the only pollinators; many other insects do the job as well. For many plants, any insect that visits the flower, such as hoverflies, will act as a pollinator (Figure 2.5). Macro organisms we can see, such as bees and butterflies, if we are persistent, we can even count. This can give us the number of individual plants and animals that we might come across in a meadow. But the health of a field, any field, depends on more than just the plants and animals that exist above ground. The flora

Figure 2.4. *Bumblebees,* **Bombus***, are superb pollinators of meadow flowers.*

Figure 2.5. *Hoverflies such as these act as pollinators on a wide range of flowers, here on devil's-bit scabious* (**Succisa pratensis**, *left) and greater knapweed* (**Centaurea scabiosa**, *right).*

and fauna of the soil itself is crucial for the long-term survival of plants and animals that live in a field. Indeed, it would not be pushing the idea too far to say that the maintenance of soil health has long-term implications for the health of the planet, and that includes us. With the change from a working field, or a chemically treated lawn, to a meadow something rather interesting can be expected to take place below ground level. The soil flora and fauna will develop and change along with the plants and animals above ground. These changes will predominantly be associated with a change in the balance of composition among the species already there. It will also involve recruiting new species from spores landing and finding a new home, much as plant seeds may drop in from passing birds, or come in on the wind. There may also be long dormant species in the soil that find the new activity of deep-rooted plants stimulating to their development. Changes in soil biodiversity that originate from a more sensitive approach to the land can also benefit surrounding gardens or fields by spreading through airborne spores and seeds.

One of the most significant changes to soil that can be found comes about as the result of a change from an agriculture that has a high anti-fungal and insecticide input to a meadow system that does not. The effects of insecticides on the biodiversity and health of an early-stage meadow is self-evident – fewer insects. But anti-fungal activity can have long-term and unseen results. Besides the need for healthy fungal flora to maintain a good soil profile, deeper and more significant changes can be brought about inadvertently. This damage, accidental or not, comes from the perceived need for farms to be able to control pests and disease. Organic farms are allowed to use pyrethrin pesticides to control insects, as long as they are plant derived. These are generally extracted from species of chrysanthemum, but wherever they come from, they are still toxic to insects, other invertebrates and fish. They operate by a process of stopping nerves from re-polarising, thereby causing paralysis. It is because they are general insecticides that any that drift onto your meadow from adjacent land will cause you problems. This may not be immediately obvious as it will manifest itself as a reduction in pollinators with a similar reduction in seed production.

When it comes to the fungal flora of the soil, the situation can be more complicated and an unwanted legacy of past actions. If we look at the fungicide regarded as acceptable for organic culture, we can see where a lot of accumulated problems can arise. The fungicide that is allowed on organic farms is called Bordeaux Mixture, a solution of $CuSO_4$ and $Ca(OH)_2$. In words, this is a solution of copper sulphate and calcium hydroxide. In the presence of a germinating fungal spore, this solution causes the release of Cu^{2+}, that is copper ions. It is the copper that kills the fungus before it can gain entry into the host tissue. This fungicide has an interesting history as it was originally created to control fungal disease in vines, and as it utilises the natural toxicity of a metal, developing resistance is all but impossible. There is little doubt that if this was introduced as a treatment for fungal disease of crops now it would quickly be taken off the market. That it still exists at all is because it is a recipe developed in the nineteenth century for use on the vineyards of France. Unfortunately it has been used on other crops, most notably fruit trees. Regardless of its known efficacy in controlling fungal disease before it gets a hold, the associated problems should stop its use. The first of these is that it is toxic to fish, so any leaching into watercourses is not to be welcomed. The second is that there is a long-term build-up in the soil of copper, which not only acts as a molluscicide, but inevitably kills other invertebrates, like earthworms, which are essential to a healthy soil.

The story does not stop there, of course, because this anti-fungal in the soil will kill symbiotic fungi that are an essential part of the life cycle of many plants, such as orchids, the seeds of which cannot germinate without a fungal associate. So a meadow in a field or orchard that has been treated with Bordeaux Mixture is going to have a reduced biodiversity and be a long project to reinstate to full health. The range of soil micro-organisms can be seen in Figure 2.6. These are just a small example of what can be found.

Meadows were an essential part of pre-mechanised agriculture, where even if there was not a great demand for grazing from food animals, there would be beasts of burden and animals associated with ploughing that would need bedding and fodder

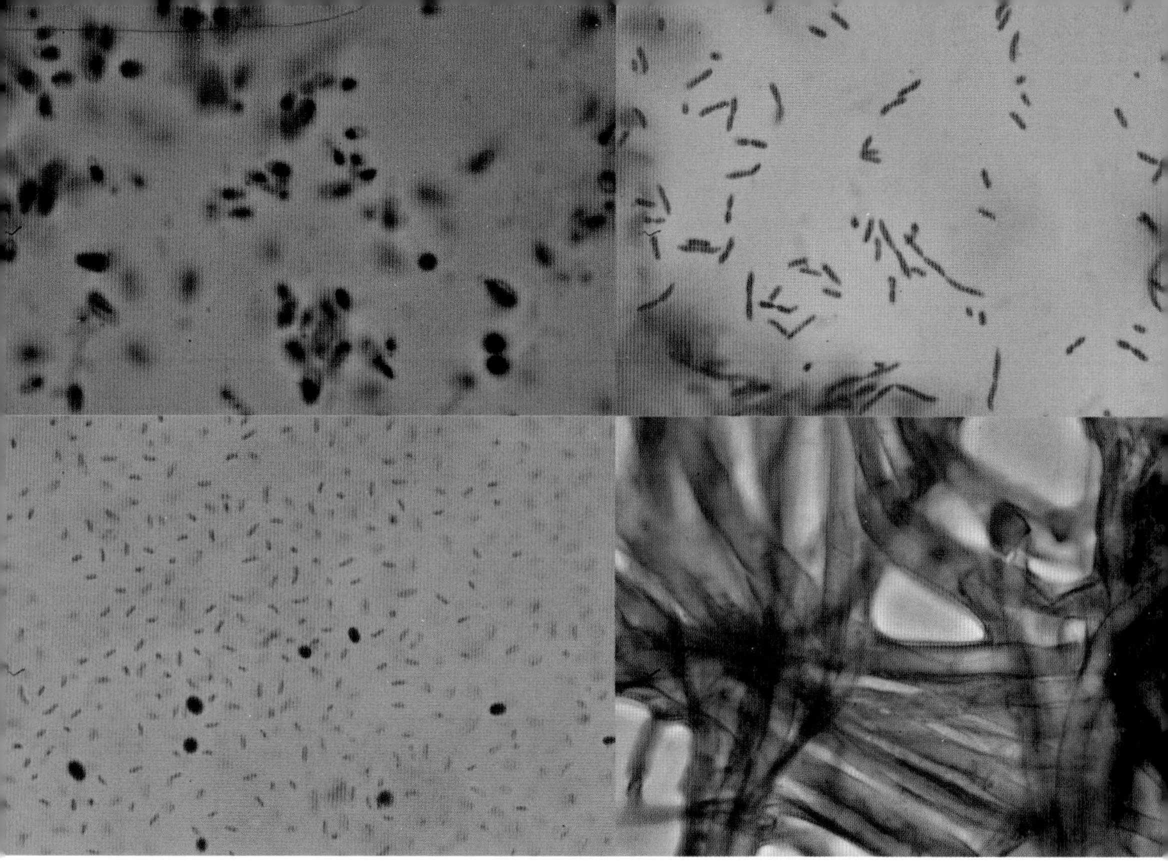

Figure 2.6. *Species of bacteria and fungi found in soil.*
a) Bacteria (top left)
b) Filamentous bacteria (top right)
c) Species of soil yeasts (bottom left).
d) Mycelium of a soil fungus (bottom right)
All these microbial forms were stained and photographed using a microscope.

throughout the winter. Once tractors were introduced and fields became bigger the perceived value of a hay meadow was reduced. While this was a natural process of changing agriculture, it was a drive for more food and cash crops in the middle of the twentieth century that really caused the downfall of meadows. The perception of them as either unproductive or low-productivity land use sounded the death knell of widespread meadow cultivation. In terms of agriculture, meadows may be seen as poor products, but we should be thinking more about the health of the planet and giving safe haven to those species that are otherwise hounded by habitat loss. If you want to, you can imagine this as being to the benefit of all those plants that need pollinators and helping to keep the soil healthy. Or you can just admit that meadows are needed, where plants and animals get on with their complex ecologies and are blissfully ignorant of the machinations of man.

Part Two

CHAPTER 3

Preparing a small garden meadow from scratch

Our small garden meadow began by accident. It started as a micro-meadow and gradually expanded to its current grand expanse of about 18 sq m. The reason? Well some thirty years ago one of us was moving house and in his garden there was a southern marsh orchid (*Dactylorhiza praetermissa*), one of those beautiful, formerly more common meadow species that are now rather rare. It was a volunteer, we think, but we don't know because it was there when he originally bought the place. Since he was selling up we thought we would try to move it to what is now the small meadow. At the time the received wisdom was that native orchids were short-lived and they do not take kindly to any form of disturbance. Nevertheless, we decided to give it a go and transplanted it in a huge divot. To our surprise, it survived and actually lived on for a long time – fifteen years in fact. It was planted up in a garden border very close to the edge of the lawn and the pond, and great care was taken not to cultivate within about 10cm of it so as not to disturb its roots.

Some four or five years later, and while watching common pondskaters (*Gerris lacustris*) on the pond, I noticed a couple of leaves in the grass that looked very orchid like. They were a bit broader than blades of grass, fleshier too and with a more rounded, hooded tip. I marked them with sticks and carefully mowed around them. The next year I had a micro-meadow with two flowering southern marsh orchids in a tiny patch with flowering grass, and with this success I did a hands and knees search of the rest of the lawn and found five or six more. Once again these were marked with sticks and mowed around. Soon it was impractical to mow around the number of orchids I marked out each year and so I left two large patches to grow into a meadow and mowed the rest. The small garden meadow was born. During this time I had also bought a couple of common spotted orchids (*Dactylorhiza fuchsii*) and planted them in the small bog garden next to our pond. These also quickly spread into the meadow. By 2014, a decade after the first volunteer southern marsh orchids flowered, there were 350 or so orchids flowering in the meadow, which is as dense as you would find in any orchid-rich traditional meadow (Figure 3.1).

Figure 3.1. *First incarnation of the small meadow, bursting with southern marsh and common spotted orchids.*

I could easily have expanded the meadow to replace the whole lawn – there were, and are, orchid leaves in the regularly mown lawn that surrounds the meadow. That I did not expand was mainly due to some rather strong domestic opposition, who wanted some lawn to sit on in the summer and was not happy with the rather scrappy look of the meadow between the flowers finishing and the hay being cut. Actually the compromise turned out to be ideal and it is one of our primary recommendations for garden meadows. A neatly cut lawn bordering the meadow enhances the meadow, rather like the mount board surrounding a watercolour. It shows that it is intentional and not just some abandoned patch of garden the owner has been too busy or too lazy to get onto. It also allows for viewing space, where you can sit in comfort and watch the goings-on without having to flatten any of the precious meadow flowers.

This initial incarnation of the small meadow was created using the first and easiest technique available to budding garden meadow makers – do nothing and let a portion of your lawn go wild. No seeds were planted. All of the flowers that made up the meadow had arrived under their own steam or were already there. The four most visually dominant were all incomers – southern marsh orchid, common spotted orchid, oxeye daisy (*Leucanthemum vulgare*) and cat's-ear (*Hypochaeris radicata*). Although the first three of them were growing in garden borders within a couple of metres of the meadow, it had taken these many years to attain dominance, and, in fact, the oxeye daisy is still invading north to south and is only about one third across.

If your only input to meadow creation is doing nothing then time is the issue. New species need to get to your meadow and the further away they are the longer it will take for chance to deliver their seed to your meadow. This is as true for small garden meadows in the suburbs as it is for large field meadows surrounded by intensively farmed land.

Even where the seed source is close, natural spread is usually very slow. When the fields in Castle Hill reserve in Sussex were taken out of cultivation and managed to return them to traditional meadows, they were fortunate to be surrounded on three sides by traditionally grazed, species-rich grassland. The management was akin to our do nothing approach, in the sense that no attempt was made to proactively add species. It involved ceasing to apply fertiliser, light grazing by cattle during the winter and taking occasional hay cuts. After ten years very few of the old chalk grassland species from the surrounding land were growing in the new meadow, despite the nearby rich seed source and such ideal management. Most new species were at the boundary, and even here the vegetation was assessed to be, at most, only one quarter of the way towards becoming like the old chalk grassland.

Why is natural spread so slow? When scientists checked out the natural seed bank – seeds buried in the top layer of soil – they found very few were from plants in the old chalk grassland and most of those were close to the boundary. The same was true for the seed rain, that is seeds falling onto the soil. This may seem strange. Plants have clever adaptations for dispersing seed over some distance, right? We are all familiar with dandelion (*Taraxacum* agg.) parachutes, thistledown, kids throwing arrows of wall barley (*Hordeum murinum*) to stick to each other's clothes or picking blackberries from a hedgerow and coming away covered in seeds of sticky willie (*Galium aparine*), but actually these are the exceptions not the rule. In the Czech flora, which is bigger than the British flora but with a similar make-up, the most common type of seed was the one with the poorest adaptation for dispersal. These accounted for more than half of the whole flora, and nearly three-quarters of the species typical of meadows and pastures.

Wind is probably the main vector for dispersal of these non-specialised seeds. The seed head gets shaken and the seeds drop out. How far it travels will depend on the strength of the wind, the weight of the seed and its density, basically how much air space it contains. Of the 100 or so species in our two meadows, the orchids have by far the lightest seeds. You would have to put 1.5 million of them onto the scales to balance the weight of a penny piece. And they also have the lowest density, because almost 80% of an orchid seed is air. In fact, orchid seed is one of those types that is highly adapted for dispersal. Nonetheless, in still air an orchid seed will hit the ground just two seconds after falling from a seed capsule half a metre high, which is going to be the highest that any meadow orchid species will grow and the sward height of many meadows in full flower. At twenty-two times heavier, sticky mouse-ear (*Cerastium glomeratum*) has the next lightest seed, and common vetch (*Vicia sativa*), the heaviest, is a whopping 14,000 times heavier. Perhaps it is not surprising that another study measured the dispersal distance of seeds for many chalk grassland wildflowers to be less than 3.5 metres. For these plants to move into a new meadow there would need to be a continuous corridor of suitable land between seed source and meadow, and the rate of progress would be glacial.

Once a seed has arrived in the meadow, there is no guarantee that it will be able to germinate and grow into an adult plant. Plants are prolific producers of seed but there is huge variation. At one extreme, for example, a single plant of common spotted orchid can produce 90,000 tiny seeds, while, at the other end of the scale, big-seeded yellow rattle (*Rhinanthus minor*) yields only about fifty per plant. Dandelion, perhaps more typical, carries around 200 on a seed head, so an average plant with ten flowers will produce around 2,000 seeds. There is simply not enough room on the planet for every seed to grow into an adult plant, and it must be the case that for most species fewer than 1 in a 1,000 do so. Most of those that do not make it either fail to germinate or die as young seedlings, and for meadow plants this is often because of competition from the plants that are already well established. Competition is exacerbated by increasing soil fertility.

There is a famous experiment in plant ecology that has run at Rothamsted Experimental Station for 150 years or more. The Park Grass Experiment started in order to find out how fertiliser treatment would affect hay yield. In 1856 a large meadow was sub-divided into a grid of plots and each plot was given a different fertiliser treatment. Every year since then the plots have been given that same treatment but for everything else they have been managed in exactly the same way. And every year the hay harvest has been weighed. The hay harvest is taken in June and, since 1875, aftermath grazing has been replaced by a second cut. Actually we are not interested in the hay yield, but we are interested in what has happened to the species diversity. The first couple of years saw a dramatic change in species composition but it took forty years to reach equilibrium in terms of the proportion of grasses, legumes (wild flowers of the pea family) and other wild flowers. Change in species composition is still happening. Any plots fertilised with nitrogen were soon taken over by grasses. They became 90% dominant. Legumes became abundant on plots given phosphate and potassium but not nitrogen. The plots with the most diversity were those that were not given any fertiliser. Even by 1860 the number of species had dropped by as much as 40% on some nitrogen-fertilised plots. Broadly speaking this is because the nitrogen encourages more vigorous grass growth and the wild flowers lose out in the competition for light. To this day, in the unfertilised plots, 'individual plants are small, and species coexist in a fine-grained, herb-rich community'.

The problem of soil that is too fertile has made one wild flower key to meadow making. Yellow rattle, which we like to call Nature's Lawnmower, is a very distinctive plant with narrow, dark green leaves and yellow tubular flowers that poke out from pale green bladder-like sepal tubes (Figure 3.2). When the seeds inside ripen and the 'bladder' dries out, the flower heads rattle as you brush past them or in the wind. Its importance to meadow making stems from its way of life; it is a partial parasite. As well as producing its own food by photosynthesis, it gets most of its water and nutrients and a substantial amount of carbon from surrounding plants by attaching its roots to theirs. The upshot generally is a reduction in the vigour of the surrounding vegetation, allowing slower-growing species to establish in the meadow and so increasing its diversity. This debilitating effect of yellow rattle on its hosts can be very large and very quick. Total meadow biomass can be reduced by up to 50%, with a significant effect apparent in just a couple of months. The biggest effect is on grasses as a group, but yellow rattle actually parasitises a very wide range of plants, perhaps most species in the meadow, even other plants of yellow rattle. We talk more about yellow rattle later, but there are two important points for now: yellow rattle itself has difficulty competing when the soil is very fertile and, because of its biology, it is able to germinate and establish in closed turf providing it is not too tall.

Figure 3.2. *Nature's Lawnmower, yellow rattle.*

Figure 3.3. *Meadow sown from standard mix in full flower.*

These days there is a wide choice of specialist meadow seed mixes, with or without grasses, from a number of suppliers. These mixes will provide you with a beautiful, bright, colourful, insect-friendly meadow in very short order (Figure 3.3). The first year will probably be a bit quiet because it will take a while for the perennials to get going. For this reason many of the mixes contain common poppy (*Papaver rhoeas*) or cornflower (*Centaurea cyanus*), which are not meadow plants at all, but they are annuals and they will add an extra splash of colour in that first year. You can get mixes suitable for sandy soils, loam soils, clay soils, calcareous soils, and more. Each mix averages twenty to thirty species. You can also get the same or very similar mixes of wildflowers with seed of grasses included, although, with these, you will be sowing fewer wildflower seeds, by as much as two-thirds when sown at the recommended density, compared with the pure wild flower mixes. And, going by the species' seed weight and the proportion of the species' seeds in the mix, some species will have very few seeds when sown at the recommended density, especially in the mixes that include grass. Remember too that germination can be poor (we discuss this more in Chapter 4). If you are only turning a small area into meadow, you may not get plants of all of the species included in your mix, and you almost certainly will not get them all if you are just broadcasting the seed onto existing turf.

So, the best use for seed mixes is to sow onto prepared bare ground. If you are starting from a completely new, 'brown' field site, perhaps turning a border into meadow or in a new house, then first the area should be prepared and levelled very much as you would do for a lawn, except that it is important not to add any fertiliser. If you are converting part of an existing lawn or an area of rough grass, you can prepare a bare surface by mowing or strimming short and then killing off the existing vegetation by covering the area with black plastic or old carpet for a few weeks. We recommend not using a herbicide because of the damage this could do to the nature you are trying to encourage. A very light cultivation of the surface layer, perhaps no more than a vigorous action with a steel spring-tine rake, will help the seeds to establish better. Remember to keep the surface moist while the seeds are germinating and afterwards for a few weeks until the seedlings become well established.

An alternative to seed mixes for creating a meadow on bare ground or where turf already exists is by laying new wild flower turf. Preparation for bare ground is the same. For existing lawn or rough grass, the surface turf must be cut away and replaced with the new turf. This is quicker and easier to do, and you have a more guaranteed establishment of the wild flowers. The first year will still be quite quiet because the turf is actually quite young, perhaps only six weeks or so in the making. On the downside, there is a smaller range of types of off-the-shelf turf available, you may have difficulty finding a supplier prepared to supply small areas and, as you would expect, they are much more expensive.

What do you do if you want to convert your lawn into a meadow without having to clear it down to bare earth and then sow seed or lay wild flower turf, but equally you do not want to wait decades for the wild flowers to turn up? The best way is to add wild flower plug plants. These are readily available with the same species as are included in the seed mixes. Of course, they are more expensive but, like turf, success is much more guaranteed. A bulb planter or sod cutter is useful for cutting out a divot of turf ready to plant the plug. Try to plant them at random to look more natural. This means having the occasional group of closely spaced plants of the same species. Of course, you can save money by making your own plug plants by buying packets of seed of individual species, germinating them, pricking out and growing on in plug plant trays. If you are on a really tight budget, you could make them from a wild flower seed mix. Germinate them in a couple of large seed trays and prick out some of each different-looking type of seedling. You will not know what they are but it will be a nice surprise when they flower.

If you do not want the expense or fuss of plug plants and are determined simply to scatter seeds, cut the existing turf as short as you can, and rake out as much thatch as you can. The more bare soil you expose, the better.

With all of these methods of creating a meadow, unless your soil is very infertile, you should always plant yellow rattle. In fact, you should probably buy extra seed even if yellow rattle is included in your mix. It is always best to sow seed and to do so in the autumn since yellow rattle requires several months of cold to trigger germination. Plug plants are not an advantage for yellow rattle, because they will already have started to parasitise the host grass that is included in the plug and will not, therefore, have so much effect on the grasses in your meadow. Ironically, since it is an annual, the plug plant's biggest effect will be after it is dead, from its seed that germinates the following year.

Everything we have described so far should lead to a colourful wild flower meadow and that is absolutely fine, isn't it? Well, yes, except that there is a certain uniformity. Back in Chapter 1, we suggested that one of the most enticing features of traditional meadows is the varied combinations of flowers and grasses to be seen in different parts of the country. There are, after all, nearly 400 species of grassland plant in Britain, more than 300 of them wild flowers. The standard turf and seed mixes only have about twenty species of wild flower in each, and only about sixty real meadow wild flowers across all of the mixes. To put it another way, all of the mixes combined only represent about 20% of the native wild flower grassland species. And, adding further to the uniformity, the same nine species are included in 75% or more of the mixes. Oxeye daisy is included in every one. This is of concern to the guardians of our native flora, organisations such as Plantlife and the Wildlife Trusts, for many reasons. For example, the seeds may originally have been sourced abroad, potentially introducing a different genotype into the native population and affecting associated species, such as insects, if, say, that genotype flowers at a different time. Similarly, species may be being planted outside their natural range so there arises confusion as to what is the natural range. Another problem can arise if vigorous agricultural varieties are used, because they are cheaper than the native variety and so, again, the native gene pool could be compromised. There is no doubt that these meadows are beautiful and they are great mini wildlife reserves, but, in our view, they don't really capture the essence of the traditional wildlife meadow. They do not have local character.

The next phase for the small meadow was to try to introduce more diversity of wild flowers. This was especially prompted when a blight got into the orchids and decimated them. In two years they went from 350 flowering spikes to none (Figure 3.4). As a botanist friend of mine joked, 'that's the trouble with mono-cultures'. For the first couple of years, my introductions were rather random, just species that I fancied in the meadow. Snake's-head fritillary (*Fritillaria meleagris*), for example. I was so taken with the fritillaries in North Meadow at Cricklade that I added some of these into the small meadow. After all, I reasoned, my small garden meadow is the next best thing to a water meadow as it is under water for much of January and February. This scattergun approach also saw cowslip (*Primula veris*) and bulbous buttercup (*Ranunculus bulbosus*) added to the meadow. The problem with the whatever-takes-your-fancy method of planting a meadow is that if the conditions,

Figure 3.4. *The small meadow after the loss of the orchids. Still a-buzz with bees.*

such as management, soil moisture, soil pH, fertility etc, do not suit the species you are trying to add, then the chances are that they will not persist. Meadow gardening is different to regular gardening: it is much more hands off. You cannot mollycoddle individual plants and if they cannot keep up with their neighbours they will die out. The small meadow is really too wet for bulbous buttercup and yet not wet enough for the fritillaries. Both have struggled and seem to be dying out. The verdict is out for cowslip, but typically it likes drier conditions than the small meadow offers. More recently, with this issue in mind, I have been trying to get more local colour into the meadow, to adjust the species composition so that it is closer to what a traditional meadow would have looked like in this area. I decided that this would be best achieved by first getting the management right and then by figuring out the species that would have grown in it.

Management is so important for determining meadow outcomes, just as it is for outcomes in every habitat, because in Britain nowhere is truly wild, untouched by man. Each plant species will respond more or less uniquely to the combination of treatments and the timing of their application. For meadows the three main types of treatment are the hay cut, grazing and fertilising. Obviously the hay cut can exclude species or at least severely limit their spread if it is timed so that it removes flower heads before seed has been set. Often the recommendation for conservation meadows is to cut the hay late in August or even early September. This may be fine for most species, allowing them to flower and set seed before the cut. It would be a disaster for the glorious Wharfedale meadow in the grounds of the old TB hospital near Grassington (Figure 1.4). In August this is awash with the hazy blue flowers of devil's-bit scabious (*Succisa pratensis*) and it sets seeds late. When it is not flowering devil's-bit scabious is not a tall plant, just a big leafy rosette that will escape the worst of a cut, while the leafless flower stalks expand late in the summer after the normal hay time in Wharfedale.

Reinstating grazing has been shown to increase the number of species in meadows in many studies and, vice versa, ceasing grazing has been found to reduce meadow diversity. I remember well visiting a reserve in the Cotswolds that was proud of its green-winged orchids (*Anacamptis morio*). Fenced off from grazing, the reserve's grass had become coarse and long and there were only one or two orchids on display. Next door in a field grazed short, there were patches where green had been turned purple by massed orchid flowers. The benefit of autumn and spring grazing comes from keeping the sward reasonably short to reduce competition for light from grasses growing on warm autumn days and also from some poaching or gap creation by heavy hooves to make space for germination.

So, how might the small meadow have been managed back when it was part of a big meadow on a traditional farm? We are lucky because there is a diary written by a local farmer in the late eighteenth century that tells all. Before the houses around here were built in the 1930s, the small meadow was in the middle of a large field, then called Meadow Flat, on the farm adjacent to that for which we have the diary. The diary entries for those types of work that affect the land, like ploughing and harvesting, are shown in Figure 3.5. Some of the diary entries are particularly significant for meadows. Mowing the hay started during the first three weeks of July and finished during the last two weeks of July or the first week of August. The difference in timing between years presumably reflects the weather. It is no good cutting the hay when it is wet and the mown hay must dry before it can be stored. After the meadows had been mowed, muck was spread on them to maintain fertility and encourage the second

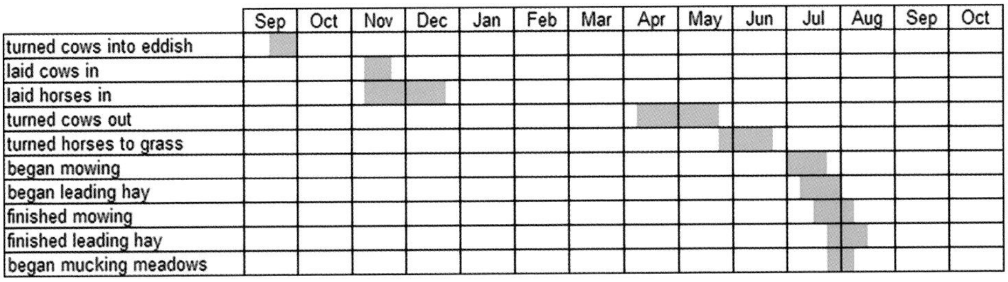

Figure 3.5. *The meadow farming year for local farmer Peter Pownall in the 1780s. The diagram shows the spread of timings for Peter's meadow management activities over the six years of the diary, starting with turning grazers out onto the aftermath and finishing with cutting and carting the hay. The events of turning the cows and horses outdoors are shown just to indicate how much of the year the grazers were indoors and eating hay.*

flush of growth. Later in the year, when the cut meadows had had their second flush of growth (the aftermath or eddish in older usage), the cows were turned out to graze on them. This happened sometime during the last two weeks of September, and they were left to graze on the meadows until being brought indoors in mid-November.

Given the sensitivity of species composition to management, it is unlikely that we will ever be able to entirely recreate a traditional meadow without using the traditional management practices and timings. Of course, realistically, this is not going to happen, especially in a garden meadow, so we have to look for alternatives that mimic those practices as closely as possible. For the small meadow, the 'management plan' is now:

1. No fertiliser to be applied. Actually, for the small meadow, this goes for the lawn that surrounds it as well. However, there is no problem if you want to treat your lawn if you leave a small untreated zone, say a half metre wide, around the meadow.
2. One hay cut a year sometime during the first three weeks of July or as soon as the orchids have set seed. My technique for the hay cut is first using a small scythe with a handle the size of a golf club (Figure 3.6). This takes off the seed heads and flower spikes and some of sward, but it is not capable of doing the full cut. This cut is left on the meadow to dry for two or three sunny days, tossing it about every day to scatter all of the seeds. Then it is raked off and the meadow is mown with a lawn mower with its catcher on to collect all of the clippings and set at its highest cut (about 2.5cm). If you do not have a scythe, you could beat the seed heads with something like a stout bamboo cane or broom handle.

The next two are my replacement for aftermath grazing:

3. A second cut with a lawn mower, again with high blades and catching clippings, during last two weeks of September. If we have an Indian summer and October is warm, a third cut may be needed at the end of the month.
4. Trample lightly over winter. This involves walking across the meadow on the heels of wellie boots whenever I am out in the garden.

Most garden meadows should be looked after like this. The main variation will be in the timing of the hay cut and the 'aftermath grazing'. These will depend on the timing of seed set and flower stalk extension for the majority of your wild flowers or for those species that you are most interested in. This is especially important for meadows with a high proportion of annuals or short-lived perennials.

Now we have the management right, how do we decide what plants to include in our traditional, local meadow? One possibility is to take some summer strolls along your

Figure 3.6. *Hay cut in the small meadow.*

nearest country lanes and footpaths and check out what is flowering on the verges or along the path borders. A very enjoyable activity, for sure, but remember that verges tend to be very fertile places, having picked up nutrients from the dust sprayed onto them by passing car tyres and fertiliser run-off from the adjacent farmland. If the vegetation is more than half a metre high, those are not the flowers you are looking for. A much better approach is to check out your county Wildlife Trust and visit any meadow reserves it has near to you in May, June and July (Figure 3.7). Another method is to visit your library and see if you can get hold of the county flora, a book written by dedicated botanists that describes all of the wild flowers that can be found or used to be found, where they are, how common they are or were and often a summary of the typical plants for the habitats found in the county. Most counties have a flora. And then it is possible to construct your own species list from scratch using the Ellenberg values we talked about in Chapter 1. Decide how your meadow rates for soil moisture, pH and fertility, and match these to the values for the meadow plants. This is made easy if you can find tables like those in the wonderful *Meadows* book by George Peterken. He groups the top 200 or so meadow plants according to

Figure 3.7. *A local meadow.*

their Ellenberg values for moisture and pH, and marks those typical of fertile soils and those that are particularly common.

I used all of these techniques to come up with my list, but especially the last. I estimate that the small meadow has Ellenberg values between 5 and 6 for moisture and between 5 and 6 for pH, and is only moderately fertile – I know that the meadow has not been fed for at least thirty years. I took the common plants from the complete table and all of the plants in the 5:5, 5:6, 6:5 and 6:6 moisture:pH groups as my starting point, then weeded out all plants marked as high fertility, all of the common plants for whom the meadow would not be wet enough, and any plant that would not normally be found in this area. You can check this out online using the distribution maps published by the Botanical Society of Britain and Ireland; the details are in the Resources section.

The final list had thirty species, half of which were already growing in the meadow, and two-thirds of those were volunteers – they had arrived under their own steam.

ALREADY IN MEADOW	TO BE ADDED
Wild flowers	
Common bird's-foot trefoil (*Lotus corniculatus*)	Autumn hawkbit (*Scorzoneroides autumnalis*)
Common mouse-ear (*Cerastium fontanum*)	Betony (*Betonica officinalis*)
Common sorrel (*Rumex acetosa*)	Changing forget-me-not (*Myosotis discolor*)
Creeping buttercup (*Ranunculus repens*)	Common dog violet (*Viola riviniana*)
Daisy (*Bellis perennis*)	Devil's-bit scabious (*Succisa pratensis*)
Dandelion (*Taraxacum* agg.)	Eyebright (*Euphrasia* agg.)
Germander speedwell (*Veronica chamaedrys*)	Knapweed (*Centaurea nigra*)
Lady's smock (*Cardamine pratensis*)	Lesser stitchwort (*Stellaria graminea*)
Meadow buttercup (*Ranunculus acris*)	Meadow saxifrage (*Saxifraga granulata*)
Red clover (*Trifolium pratense*)	Meadow vetchling (*Lathyrus pratensis*)
Selfheal (*Prunella vulgaris*)	Pale lady's-mantle (*Alchemilla xanthochlora*)
Thyme-leaved speedwell (*Veronica serpyllifolia*)	Pignut (*Conopodium majus*)
White clover (*Trifolium repens*)	Ribwort plantain (*Plantago lanceolata*)
Yellow rattle (*Rhinanthus minor*)	Tufted vetch (*Vicia cracca*)
	Yarrow (*Achillea millefolium*)
Grasses	
Common bent (*Agrostis capillaris*)	Glaucous sedge (*Carex flacca*)
Crested dog's-tail (*Cynosurus cristatus*)	Pale sedge (*Carex pallescens*)
Field wood-rush (*Luzula campestris*)	Red fescue (*Festuca rubra*)
Meadow foxtail (*Alopecurus pratensis*)	
Rough meadow-grass (*Poa trivialis*)	
Sweet vernal grass (*Anthoxanthum odoratum*)	
Yorkshire fog (*Holcus lanatus*)	

Interestingly, only about half of the species, around ten, in a typical packet of wildflower seed suitable for the soil conditions in the small meadow are on the final list. However, all but three of the to-be-added species are available as seeds from commercial wild flower specialist suppliers.

Another fourteen species not on the final list are growing in the meadow, a mixture of garden escapes that probably will not survive, my whatever-takes-your-fancy species that probably will not survive and volunteers that may well have been found in a local meadow, especially cat's-ear, which currently dominates the meadow and the two orchid species.

The plan is to add plug plants or seeds of the to-be-added species that are available and watch what happens. In theory the meadow will come to an equilibrium where the plants that are not suitable will die out. Only garden lady's-mantle (*Alchemilla mollis*), one of the volunteers coming in from the border, will be controlled if it turns out to be too vigorous.

This sort of approach can be used for a garden meadow anywhere. If you are starting from bare soil it is probably best to start with a commercial seed mix. As we have seen, these tend to contain the most common species, they are all quite similar, and even the one most closely matched to your conditions might only have ten or so of the species you actually want. However, they will give you good coverage and a very pretty meadow that you can use as a starting point for crafting your own local version. An attractive alternative to known mixes is to use undefined mixes harvested from existing traditional meadows. In these mixes you are guaranteed to get at least some seed of the main species in the meadow but which of the minor species are included is pot luck. To our mind this is the best solution as a starter pack if you can get seed from a meadow that matches your conditions. There is great excitement in seeing what turns up and you may get some unusual species that are not easily available anywhere else.

We know that the most reliable way of establishing new species in your existing meadow is to use plug plants. You can create these yourself from seed packets and for most plants this will be the best approach. Some, however, are better sown directly into the meadow. The tiny seed of orchids, for example, is parasitic on fungi for the first year or so of its life. This is actually an advantage for orchid establishment because it means that the orchid can get to a good size before it appears above ground and starts to compete with the surrounding vegetation. In a pot, you may not have the required fungus in your potting compost, and, anyway, an orchid will not appear, if it is going to at all, for at least eighteen months.

Pignut is another example. It will need two or three years in a pot before it is ready to plant out (Figure 3.8). Pignut has an unusual morphology. Its two seed leaves (cotyledons) are fused together and in its first year all that appears above ground is this tiny fused seed leaf, looking very much like a very thin blade of grass. The second year plant is just a single, small, finely divided leaf the size of a five pence piece. At the end of the third year the 'nut', actually a tuber, has grown into a small bulb about the size of a snowdrop, and this is the best thing to plant out in the autumn. Because of this fuss, we suggest that it is best to sow pignut directly into the meadow in the first place. If you are not sure which seeds are better turned into plug plants and which sown directly into the meadow, split your seed packet into two and try both. If you are planting seeds into the meadow, do it when the soil is moist and try rubbing them into the soil rather than just scattering them. Also try closely cropping the immediately surrounding turf. If you are planting plug plants use a bulb planter or sod plugger to remove a small section of turf. The danger of removing a small divot is that you may be removing a special plant, because after the hay harvest in the autumn or before growth really gets going in the spring it is easy to forget exactly where your special meadow plants are. The best way around this is to mark the position of special plants, or the places where it is safe to plant plugs, whichever is the fewest, just before the hay cut. You can use golf tees, which are bright and visible but low enough to escape the scythe or mower.

As well as commercial suppliers of seeds and plug plants, it is possible to source commoner plants by collecting seed or, in some cases, taking cuttings. If the plant is on private land you should always get the landowner's permission, and you should only ever take a small portion of the seed, just enough to enable you to grow a few

Figure 3.8. *Two-year-old plants of pignut.*

plug plants. You should not be collecting enough to sow a whole meadow. Similarly, if the plant can be grown from cuttings, take just a few to make stock plants and bulk up from them. Please do not dig up plants. In most cases it is against the law to do this but more importantly it goes against everything we are trying to do – we aim to increase our wildlife, not reduce it.

Do not be despondent if your first attempts to increase diversity do not work. Almost every study has found there is a gradual loss of species over the first few years following meadow creation and it is likely that sometimes plants introduced in only small numbers will be lost. When there are only a few plants of a species in a meadow they will always be at risk of dying out, especially if the species is an annual or short-lived perennial. With only a few plants, pollination is probably not going to be very efficient. If the young plants are struggling they will not produce so many flowers nor as much seed and, if they are perennials, they will not be able to store so much food for the following year, when they may succumb to competition from the fitter individuals around them. Clearly, if a plant doesn't quite fit the combination of environment and management it is not going to survive, but, if you think the plants you have added should be the right ones for the meadow, be prepared to try again. Some plants will need several attempts before they establish, perhaps because the meadow is gradually changing and competition changes. It is fascinating to try to figure out what is going on and tremendously exciting when things do work out, as they have for the small meadow. Its orchids are gradually coming back.

All this fussiness is fine for a small garden meadow, it is actually less effort than you would normally put into the rest of the garden, and, to our minds, for much greater reward. When it comes to larger areas, though, it becomes untenable. So how do you create or restore a full-sized meadow? This is what we explore in the next chapter.

CHAPTER 4

Setting up a large field meadow, from scratch and as a restoration

Large meadows generally follow along the same lines as a garden meadow, except the range of species can be many times greater. Among species that can be found in larger meadows that do not usually take up residence in gardens are lagomorphs – rabbits (*Oryctolagus cuniculus*) and brown hares (*Lepus europaeus*), foxes (*Vulpes vulpes*), badgers (*Meles meles*) and if there is some rough scrub for cover, deer. The difference, as you can see, is the need for larger mammals to have more space and cover in which to make a home. Setting up, or restoring, a larger meadow also has the drawbacks of having larger mammals present. While rabbits will generally scrape small depressions and holes, badgers especially will dig large holes and deer seem to love eating flowers. In the large meadow we quite often find cowslips (*Primula veris*) with the flower heads neatly nipped off, and orchids where the flowers have been taken off, leaving a standing stalk denuded of flowers. The presence of rabbits will result in a lot of digging, with scrapes and holes appearing all over the place. These are not necessarily as destructive as you may at first imagine as they produce areas of bare soil that can be colonised by species that have trouble seeding into a continuous greensward.

It is always a valuable starting point to decide what type of field flora you have. For this, it is worth getting a guide to wild flowers to see how many you can identify. Once you have a list of plants and an idea of numbers you can use the following key to determine what actions need to be taken.

This is a dichotomous key for determining if you have species-rich grassland.

Start at the top with number 1 and answer the questions **yes** or **no.** Each answer will take you to the next stage and eventually help you to identify the type of grassland that you have. This does not follow the lengthy and complicated British National Vegetation Classification (BNVC), which, as we discussed in Chapter 1, is too complex for our purposes.

With this very simple key we are going to help you decide whether you have a **species-rich grassland**, a **semi-improved grassland**, **improved grassland**, or some

other habitat that is not strictly grassland at all, such as heath. The grassland types are broadly lowland neutral, acidic or calcareous (limestone). The flora of these three varies, but determining the status of a plot follows the same route. Improvement levels refer to the agricultural potential, so a highly improved pasture is usually an almost perennial rye-grass (*Lolium perenne*) monoculture.

If you are unsure of plant identification it is worth trying to arrange a botanical survey to ascertain the dominant species and numbers of species present.

1. Cover by perennial rye-grass, creeping buttercup (*Ranunculus repens*) and white clover (*Trifolium repens*) is *less* than 10% and there are more than fifteen species of wild flower/sq m.
   If **YES** then go to 7.
   If **NO** then go to 2.
2. Cover by perennial rye-grass, creeping buttercup and white clover is *less* than 30% and there are more than eight species of wild flower/sq m, covering more than 10% of the ground and including grasses other than perennial rye-grass.
   If **YES** then go to 4.
   If **NO** then go to 3.
3. Cover by perennial rye-grass, creeping buttercup and white clover is *more* than 30%, with no more than eight wild flower species/sq m and these wild flowers, excluding white clover and creeping buttercup, covering no more than 10% of the ground.
   If **YES** then go to 5.
   If **NO** then go to 6.
4. This indicates that your plot is most likely to be a *semi-improved grassland*. This often contains the same indicator species as are found in *species-rich grassland* but at lower levels. For the indicator species see the lists for the different grassland types below. The species that are present may be in patches and rather sporadic. Semi-improved grassland is ideal for restoration.
5. This indicates a species-poor *improved grassland*. It has probably had applications of fertilisers that will need to be reduced and is more of a creation project than a restoration.
6. Your field may not be a grassland, it may be a marsh or heathland, which are not normally suitable as meadows as they have their own ecology.
7. This indicates grassland that is already *species-rich*. It would benefit from careful management, but it would be best to continue with the previous management that brought it to this condition. There are three broad forms of species-rich meadow that are determined by their soil, but can be separated by their flora. The species and abundance will vary depending upon wetness and latitude as well as soil type, but the meadow is likely to have a good number

of the following that are typical for the soil type. Although these lists are not exhaustive, they are indicative of what might be found.

Neutral grassland

Agrimony (*Agrimonia eupatoria*), common bird's-foot trefoil (*Lotus corniculatus*), common spotted orchid (*Dactylorhiza fuchsii*), cowslip, crested dog's-tail (*Cynosurus cristatus*), dyer's greenweed (*Genista tinctoria*), glaucous sedge (*Carex flacca*), green-winged orchid (*Anacamptis morio*), knapweed (*Centaurea nigra*), lady's bedstraw (*Galium verum*), meadow saxifrage (*Saxifraga granulata*), oxeye daisy (*Leucanthemum vulgare*), pepper-saxifrage (*Silaum silaus*), red clover (*Trifolium pratense*), rough meadow-grass (*Poa trivialis*), smooth meadow-grass (*Poa pratensis*) and yellow rattle (*Rhinanthus minor*)

Calcareous grassland

Bee orchid (*Ophrys apifera*), chalk fragrant orchid (*Gymnadenia conopsea*), chalk milkwort (*Polygala calcarea*), common spotted orchid (*Dactylorhiza fuchsii*), twayblade (*Neottia ovata*), downy oat-grass (*Avenula pubescens*), dwarf thistle (*Cirsium acaule*), fairy flax (*Linum catharticum*), field scabious (*Knautia arvensis*), greater knapweed (*Centaurea scabiosa*), hairy violet (*Viola hirta*), hoary plantain (*Plantago media*), pyramidal orchid (*Anacamptis pyramidalis*), quaking grass (*Briza media*), rough hawkbit (*Leontodon hispidus*), salad burnet (*Poterium sanguisorba*), upright brome (*Bromopsis erecta*), wild carrot (*Daucus carota*) and yellow oat-grass (*Trisetum flavescens*)

Acidic grassland

Betony (*Betonica officinalis*), cat's-ear (*Hypochaeris radicata*), common bent (*Agrostis capillaris*), field wood-rush (*Luzula campestris*), harebell (*Campanula rotundifolia*), heath bedstraw (*Galium saxatile*), heath spotted orchid (*Dactylorhiza maculata*), lady's smock (*Cardamine pratensis*), lesser butterfly orchid (*Platanthera bifolia*), lesser stitchwort (*Stellaria graminea*), lousewort (*Pedicularis sylvatica*), pignut (*Conopodium majus*), sheep's fescue (*Festuca ovina*), sheep's sorrel (*Rumex acetosella*), sweet vernal grass (*Anthoxanthum odoratum*) and tormentil (*Potentilla erecta*)

Before going on to create a large meadow it would be worth looking at methods of restoration as this tends to be a more gentle process than starting one from scratch. At the same time, many of the techniques that are used in restoration projects can be used directly in meadow creation. With either sort of project it is important to assess what you have and what you may need to do before starting a meadow project. This serves two purposes. The first is to put into perspective the amount of time you will require and the second is how much money you are likely to need to put into the project. With a large project it is worth investigating whether you could apply for a stewardship grant. These are administered by the government body Natural England. In our Resources section we have several useful addresses for grant bodies and suppliers of machinery, help and advice.

As described in Chapter 3, even small meadows, and certainly large ones, benefit from being seeded with yellow rattle (Figure 4.1) and there is more on the biology of how this species works in Chapter 5. As this is a pivotal species for many meadow types, it is worth looking at it and its husbandry in some detail. Primary seeding with yellow rattle does not need to be on a large scale as this plant seeds easily and spreads quite well on its own. The importance of this species stems from its life cycle, in which it has a preference for parasitising grass. It does not need the host species, but if it is there it will take advantage. It is especially comfortable growing in conjunction with grasses and legumes, although it will happily attach to other wildflower species. The main purpose of having yellow rattle is to control grasses, a job it does very well by reducing the growth of these plants. It will, however, have trouble in establishing itself in a sward that has been intensively managed, where the dominant species is likely to be perennial rye-grass (*Lolium perenne*), because of competition. One of the interesting aspects of yellow rattle is that it has been used as a target species for beekeepers to make honey, and from personal experience the result is very good. The spreading of yellow rattle can be a slower process than you might like, so when you make your hay cut, take some of the clippings from an area that is well provided with the species and strew them over

Figure 4.1. *In our meadow the yellow rattle grows and seeds unaided, so long as the plants have set seed before the autumn cut.*

the areas less well provided for. The method that we have found best for doing this is by having a high-density seeding area as an original stock source. Once cut, enough seed will have dropped to keep it fully stocked, and at the same time, there will be enough seed material left to take the clipped foliage and distribute it elsewhere in the meadow.

Yellow rattle is a species that has a wide range of tolerance for soil types, so it is a natural and widespread coloniser of all types of meadows from northern hay meadows, lowland hay meadows through flood meadows to water meadows. One aspect that has been reported is that it does not normally appear when the pH is below 5, making it averse to very acidic conditions. The seed itself does not survive very long, so there is a very small natural seed bank and inappropriate cutting, before seed set, will virtually wipe out the entire population. Seed germination takes place between February and April, depending upon the latitude, and needs a period of chilling to break dormancy. If you are buying seed from a supplier it really does need to be from that year's crop and should be put on the land as soon as possible. Rates of seeding that have been recommended range from 0.5 to 2.5kg per hectare. This is to establish a plant density for yellow rattle of between 100 and 200 plants per sq m. This is a figure predicated on a 'no patience' principle; that is creating a complete self-sustaining population density in a single year. If you are not in a tearing hurry – and we feel creating a meadow should be an evolutionary activity rather than a revolutionary one – such densities do not need to be achieved in a single season. In some reports, densities of 30kg of seed per hectare have been suggested for a high-productivity sward of improved pasture, but this makes such planting hideously expensive. A different approach is to use hay from a meadow already well stocked with yellow rattle. This is not only cheaper, but can also introduce other species of wild flowers that have seeds in with the desired yellow rattle. If you can source the meadow clippings locally you can also be sure that the mix of plants will be well suited to your field. Spreading seeds in this way may also help in not accidentally introducing inappropriate plants. This may happen with purchased yellow rattle seed, where it may have originated in parts of Europe where the very similar-looking greater yellow rattle (*Rhinanthus angustifolius*) (Figure 4.2) is the more common species.

In broad terms, scattering seed in a random or haphazard way works quite well, but if you have a large area you want to seed in a single year, a mechanical aid is a good idea. Seeding can be done using a fertiliser spreader, or a seed drill where the coulters are lifted so that the planting depth is minimal. The use of mechanical devices for seeding would only really be necessary if it is a large field being done in a single season. Generally hand sowing is enough to get the ecology moving; it is, after all, a process of setting up a system that will sustain itself and proliferate over the years. If you have a dense sward, once the seed is scattered it should be raked in, or rolled in. This can be achieved by the action of livestock in the field, but as seed is scattered in the autumn, it should be cleared of animals in February when most seed is germinating.

Figure 4.2. *Greater yellow rattle is very similar to our native yellow rattle, but uncommon in the UK and questionably native here.*

Some of the areas that you may wish to seed will probably benefit from a pre-treatment. This should result in a short sward, well below 10cm if possible, with bare patches scattered around. Although this can be created by livestock grazing, the hoof and tooth method, it has been demonstrated in many places that mechanical methods, such as a power harrow or a set of discs works very well. Although it is not a situation that I have ever seen, if your yellow rattle becomes so prolific it is taking over it is very easily controlled by cutting it while it is in flower, or by early season grazing. Concern for excessive yellow rattle usually arises from a reduction in hay yield. If you are not collecting hay for commercial use, this should not be of any particular concern. Some areas of our meadow had a sward in which the predominant species was yellow rattle, with other broad-leaved plants and very little grass. This gradually became a balanced area of great variety without controlling the rattle growth. I don't want to give the impression that yellow rattle will just keep on increasing, it is part of the ecosystem and has its own species that control it. The best known of these is a small moth, the grass rivulet (*Perizoma albulata*), that is on the wing from May to July and has a caterpillar that lives and feeds inside the seed capsule.

Restoration of meadow areas should always start with an assessment of what you have in the field that is left from the natural meadow flora and fauna. It should be obvious that while you will be manipulating the flora of your meadow, you will be simultaneously creating new habitats for wildlife of all sorts. With this in mind, if your field has any scrub or low woody growth such as brambles, before grubbing it up consider its habitat potential. Scrub areas can be of considerable value to birds and mammals, so it is worth setting up a trail camera that is motion sensitive. These are relatively inexpensive and the results can be quite a surprise. Our own area of scrubland, which we have left intact after using a camera, has demonstrated the presence of muntjac deer (*Muntiacus reevesi*), foxes, rabbits, badgers and innumerable wood mice (*Apodemus sylvaticus*). This is all in an area of no more than half an acre, but the dense scrub gives good daylight cover and night-time foraging (Figure 4.3 also Figures 8.6, 8.9 and 8.10).

When you have looked at your plot, look at surrounding fields. Even if they are not meadows themselves the degree of 'improvement' they have undergone may vary from field to field. This may give you an idea of the range of plants you can expect to grow. The type of plants that will do well will be site specific, but the overlaps are considerable between vegetation types. Introducing plants that do not appear locally does not mean they will not do well. It may be just that for reasons of lack of seed or inability to compete in a fertilised environment, or some other unknown reason, they have disappeared or never became established. By considering the existing plants in the meadow it becomes possible to decide which ones can be used as seed stock to spread around more broadly and those that should not be encouraged as they are

Figure 4.3. *You may find the range of animal species in your meadow is greater than you realise if you use a motion-sensitive camera. a) One of our foxes, which was active in daylight hours (top left). b) Wood mice, the heat from their eyes generating bright points in the image (bottom left). c) Extremely cute, very sleek and very fast, a wood mouse in daylight (right).*

transient species associated with fertiliser and agricultural pressure. Species in this category include white clover (*Trifolium repens*) and perennial rye-grass (*Lolium perenne*).

Some plant species can take on the persona of weeds if they are left, such as nettles (*Urtica dioica*) and thistles. These tend to be associated with over-grazing or more specifically grazing by horses. Horses have the tendency to use the same area for toileting, so the ground becomes highly nitrogenous, as if it had been artificially fertilised. The resultant patches of nettles can out-compete virtually all other species, so cutting them back two or even three times in a year may be necessary to limit their spread. Using this sort of intervention is not aimed at eradication, but a level of control that gives other species a chance.

If the fertility of the soil is not too high, then introducing a regular hay cut may be enough to restore the meadow to its former glory. Initially a double cut can be used, one at the end of the flowering season in the autumn and another, early spring cut, before the flowers' buds are at cutting height. As with all such cutting, it is important to take away the cut hay, even if it is just stacked in a corner. If it is left on the meadow it will just recycle nutrients back into the soil. During the early years the meadow can be used for winter grazing, but be very careful of the load and the types of animals used. Horses tend to cause considerable damage because they are metal shod and the ground in winter is very soft. They will also tend to over-graze areas as they prefer a short sward, so will stick to areas that suit them rather than straying into long grass where their cutting bite would do more good. The other aspect of winter grazing is that if you have to supply additional fodder this will be recycled into fertiliser, which will be left on the meadow.

Once the meadow has settled down with a reduced growth of grass and is ready for an increase in floral diversity, the two main options are to strew hay from a biodiverse meadow of the same sort, or to scatter seed of specific species in areas of the plot where they will be most likely to grow. On large-scale projects the idea of using plug plants should be abandoned as simply too expensive and labour intensive. For suitable hay to spread on your field, if you approach your local Wildlife Trust they may well be able to help in locating a source of meadow hay that will suit your ground.

At Castle Hill, a nature reserve in Sussex, they tested the germination and survival of four species typical of old chalk grassland on the old original site and the new meadows being recreated from the ex-arable land. They scattered seed in April, counted the number to germinate and then monitored their survival for the rest of the spring and summer. A lot of seed was scattered, enough in each plot so that, if their germination was the same as in the laboratory, 500 plants of each species would germinate. Germination was low, exceedingly so in the new meadow where only about 1 in 90 of the expected seedlings germinated, while 1 in 14 germinated on the old chalk grassland. Now, when they cut the sward in the new meadow very short (to 3cm) about 1 in 8 seeds germinated, but the best for germination was when they cleared the plots in the new meadow completely by cutting to ground level and even here only about 1 in 4 germinated.

Survival followed a similar pattern, except that seedlings fared best in the cut new meadow plots, followed in sequence by cleared new meadow plots and the old chalk grassland. This pattern of survival is to be expected. Seedlings will suffer more competition for light in sites where the surrounding vegetation is taller (old chalk grassland) but are helped by the more moderate environment created by shorter sward (cut new meadow) compared with bare land (cleared new meadow) where temperature variation is more extreme and less moisture is retained in the soil. Germination was so poor on the untreated chalk grassland plots that seedling survival could not be assessed, but we can safely assume that it was worst there. The striking message is that 500+ seeds is still not enough to establish even a single adult plant in a meadow that is not amenable to them.

It is reasonable to ask how come traditional meadows became so rich in species. After all, many of these were not decades old as farmers would relay them every now and then. There are many reasons. Foremost among them is that, one way or another, the seed came from existing meadows, often simply by sweeping the hay barn floor, and any form of seed cleaning available to them would not have been very efficient. Add to this the likely richer seed bank in the soil, depending on the previous use of the field. Also, there being many more traditional meadows, and with all mechanised farm work powered by horses, they could have carried seed into the meadows in their hooves, coats and dung.

Very similar results to those found at Castle Hill have been seen in many other studies. One of these of particular interest to us was done by Swedish conservationists when they experimented with various ways of creating amenity meadows in urban situations. They tried a multitude of potential approaches on their two sites, one clayey and the other sandy. Although the sites are drier and colder than most places in Britain, which may affect the precise balance and timeline of the results, the principles are going to be very similar. They tried sowing a wildflower seed mix in autumn or spring, onto bare soil after ploughing or existing turf, using a mulch or a nursery crop on the bare soil, and cutting or burning strips or circles of various widths into the existing turf. They also tried planting wild flower plug plants into existing turf.

They found that a nursery crop or mulch helps establishment when seeds are sown on bare ground. Rye (*Secale cereale*) was the best nursery crop they tried and hay the best mulch. A mulch gives better results than a nursery crop for autumn sowings. Both mulch and nursery crop provide some protection to young seedlings. Much like very short turf, they ameliorate the microclimate by keeping temperature more constant and retaining soil moisture. With a nursery crop the advantage of this protection is delicately balanced against the competition for light that the crop also brings. Rye-grass is too competitive and using it as a nursery crop was worse than not using a nursery crop at all. This is probably why a mulch was better for autumn sowing – if the nursery crop germinates in the autumn it is more established and therefore a better competitor for light than the spring-germinating wild flowers, and if it does not germinate until spring it cannot offer protection to autumn-germinating plants. Of the two mulches tried, hay was better than straw. This could have been because there was extra seed coming from the hay. Certainly the source of the hay mulch will be important if it does contain seed. If you are thinking of going this route, a mulch must not be from an improved meadow or grassland because this will potentially include the seed of competitive grasses.

When sowing into existing turf, the conservationists found that gaps definitely help establishment, and it makes no difference whether these are strips or circles. The wider the gap the better, although we can only say that this is true up to 10cm because that was the maximum width they tried, and creating the gap by removing turf is better than by burning it off. Again competition is the important factor here. The existing turf will grow back from being burnt off and compete with the seedlings for light, and similarly the surrounding vegetation will compete more effectively for light in narrower gaps. In this process we have been helped considerably by the action of rabbits (Figure 4.4, also 8.7).

Figure 4.4. *A rabbit dig. The area of bare earth around the hole will benefit seed germination, assuming that the seeds and seedlings are not eaten by the rabbits.*

With a few exceptions, wild flower plugs planted directly into existing turf survived well and so in a sense this is the most successful method, but also, of course, easily the most expensive. Although suitable for small plots, it is impracticable for large meadows. The survival of plug plants is probably due to overcoming the competition for light, water and nutrients from surrounding vegetation. As we have seen before, newly germinated seedlings are most likely to die during the first two weeks and plug plants have already been nursed through this risky period. The exceptions were a few species that are normally found in soils with low nutrient availability, and the study sites were probably too nutrient rich for them to keep up with the surrounding plants that could make more use of the nutrients available.

Species of the genus *Jacobaea*, the ragworts, seem to cause an almost universal chorus of 'weed' when they are mentioned, but this is to do them a disservice. These species used to be in the genus *Senecio*, together with the groundsels, but have been moved based on genetic information. Common ragwort, or usually just ragwort, referred to as *Senecio jacobaea* in older texts and as *Jacobaea vulgaris* in more modern ones, is the main offender. Whatever the current naming convention, of one thing we can be sure, ragwort is a native plant and it is not invasive; it is an opportunist coloniser, requiring as it does, bare soil for the seeds to land on. Although it is a poisonous plant when eaten, stories of it being hazardous to handle are grossly overstated. In fact, even the stories of its toxicity are generally exaggerated. These stories seem to have originated with the horse-owning part of the population. Poisoning is a potential problem mainly promulgated by horse owners, many of whom are responsible for their own crop of ragwort. The story is simple: ragwort needs access to open ground to germinate and paddocks are often so trampled and over-grazed that they create ideal conditions for ragwort growth (Figure 4.5). Besides which, seed spread is very limited, most seed drifting to the ground quite close to the parent plant. What is not often realised is that horses, along with most livestock, will avoid eating ragwort, so it is only likely to be a problem in dry hay where the bitter taste is much reduced.

Ragwort is made toxic by the presence of pyrrolizidine alkaloids, which are normally rendered damaging by digestive action in the gut. The thing here is that by all normal measures they are no worse than many other toxic wild flowers that we do not really pay very much attention to, so exactly why ragwort has been singled out for the opprobrium that it has is something of a mystery. We can be sure of one thing, though: ragwort is an important part of our native flora. It supports either directly, as in the cinnabar moth (*Tyria jacobaeae*), or indirectly, as in the common blue butterfly (*Polyommatus icarus*), in excess of 150 different invertebrate species. This is not a plant that should be vilified and dug up at every available opportunity. Something that we have found with the large meadow is that as it has developed, since grazing by horses stopped and the ground cover has increased, the number of ragwort plants has

Figure 4.5. *An area of over-grazing in the large meadow, after a year without horses the ragwort seems to have taken over.*

decreased significantly. We still have it in the meadow, with its pretty yellow flowers, and we still have cinnabar moths (Figure 4.6) as well, and that is how it should be.

It remains perplexing as to why ragwort should be singled out as a toxic hazard, especially as it is not generally grazed. There are some other toxic plants growing in our meadow margins, such as the nightshades, white bryony (*Bryonia dioica*), foxglove (*Digitalis purpurea*) and cuckoo pint (*Arum maculatum*), and we have a happy relationship with them. They all contribute to the stability of the ecosystem. When you are considering the amount of ragwort in a field, it is important to be certain of identification as, from a distance, there are other species that look very similar (Figure 4.7).

For most plants, although seed germination can be much reduced in a meadow simply because a lot of the seed will inevitably end up in the wrong place, scattering is a way of generating a system that will be self-sustaining. The reason this is in many ways better than plug planting is that if the seed germinates and grows, it is in the right place. If you plant an already germinated seed you have to trust to luck that it will take and prosper. This also applies to creating a hedge around your meadow.

By taking the long view, a hedge can be created that comprises plants in the right place. In the large meadow it was apparent that we needed a hedge along two of its sides, so we started by putting in whips of several different species, mainly hawthorn (*Crataegus monogyna*), blackthorn (*Prunus spinosa*) and field maple (*Acer campestre*). Many of these rooted saplings did not survive the first winter and following spring.

Figure 4.6. *Cinnabar moth caterpillars feasting on ragwort.*

Figure 4.7. *From a distance this bank of perforate St John's-wort,* **Hypericum perforatum**, *could be mistaken for ragwort. As we have perforate St John's-wort, we also have treble-bar moths,* **Aplocera plagiata** *(inset), which uses it as a food plant.*

Those that did survive were very slow to move and start growing, so much so, that we devised an experiment. Collecting the haws from some of the hawthorn trees in our scrub area, we laid a line of them along our proposed hedge line. This is currently an experiment in operation and will generate results over the next few years. It is that scale of time, years, that is important to take into account when developing a meadow and its boundaries. There is little point in rushing as this will skew the balance of plants and consequently the fauna as well. Your large field should be nudged towards a stable meadow, and you should allow it time to develop at its own pace. By doing this you can watch as it develops and changes with the years.

Some of the routes to a grassland meadow that have been advocated in the past, and even now are still regarded as reasonable by some, can only be described as an energy-consuming pointless short cut. What is more, they will devastate the existing and developing ecosystem of your meadow. Such methods include removal of the existing sward. This is said to be possible in one of two ways. The first is mechanical, quite literally stripping the turf and topsoil. This is extremely destructive on every single level and is a very out of fashion process. Sometimes local councils will use this technique, but mainly because they have a targeted outcome and the process is not considered in any other way than as part of an annual budget. This is in some ways strange because the cost is high and the outcome is intrinsically unsatisfactory. The second method that is best avoided is to destroy all the plant life chemically. The herbicide generally used for this is glyphosate, which is still in use in some areas. But these two techniques fly in the face of everything you want to do when setting up a meadow. By starting or restoring a meadow you are saying something about your interest in conservation and biodiversity, so why would you want to destroy what is already there just so it can be replaced by a different range of species? Far better to work with the ecosystem you have, however impoverished it is, and start to build up a new and more biodiverse system without causing unnecessary damage in the process. When you decide to turn over a field or paddock to become a meadow you will need to leave the modern philosophy of instantaneous results behind, to become far more patient with natural processes and the seasonal changes that take place at their own pace.

The large meadow was a badly maintained paddock that varied from over-grazed grass to non-grazable bracken (*Pteridium aquilinum*) (Figure 4.8). After a period of five years it had become a very much more biodiverse field of over 100 plant species and gives immense pleasure just to sit in and listen to the birds and insects.

Once established as a meadow, the ecosystem will change slowly and evolve with some input from the major grazing animal, which is you. If you skip the autumn cut you will find, as we do, that there is a tendency to develop oak scrub. This is a very specific result, because other species of tree depend on the tree being in the meadow or in the hedge line. Oak trees do not operate in this way. We do not have any oak trees either in the meadow or in the hedge, what we do have is a lot of transient magpies (*Pica pica*). We think that it is

Figure 4.8. *Starting point for a meadow, an over-grazed paddock that had been home to horses for many years.*

these noisy and distinctive birds that bring the acorns into the large meadow rather than jays (*Garrulus glandarius*), which are classically responsible for this (see Chapter 7). The birds do a fantastic job and although we try to move the seedling trees to the boundary for replanting, most of them will be trimmed in the autumn cut. This can be done by machinery or by hand and is detailed in Chapter 7.

The number of species seen in our meadow is not fixed, as new species turn up from time to time, while some species disappear for years on end, or they appear to. I say appear to because with a large plot, say larger than a hectare, the possibility of a species being there but unseen is actually quite large. Admittedly, if it is a large and flamboyant species, say a butterfly or a rose, it is difficult not to see it, but if it is something small and normally only found in low numbers, then overlooking it is very easy. This is even more likely with rare and exotic insects, where their presence might only be apparent once every couple of years, but that they turn up every now and again does indicate that they are there even when they are not seen.

One of the benefits of a species list, either plant or animal, for a large meadow is that it becomes a useful measure of change. This change can be as simple as the alterations in the biosphere of the meadow itself as it moves towards a stable agricultural system. It can demonstrate far more than this, however. If you find a species appearing in consecutive years it is reasonable to assume that it has become established, if you then think that this is a species that would not necessarily be found in this geographical area, you can be pleased with the arrival of the unusual. You may also be registering a change that had not previously been noted; a northern move of a southern species due to climate change, or one that has special habitat requirements that you have reinstated. With such actions you will have become a true conservationist.

Part Three

CHAPTER 5

Meadows in spring

Spring, in many ways like autumn, holds an odd position as while a lot is happening in the meadow, it is positioned between two far better-defined seasons, winter and summer. Spring can be seen as an artificial construction of the calendar, but there is no denying that you recognise it when it comes. The arrival of spring has an official date, 20 March, and an end date, 21 June, but nature ignores sleepy officials and their astronomical dates. The study of biological indicators of seasons is phenology and the measure of the changes of the position of seasons on a timescale lasting longer than a parliament is a very instructive way of looking at climate change. The onset of spring is especially good for this as there are specific harbingers of the growth to come that can be used as timers. The reason for this is that although daylight hours will not change year to year, temperature will and this is most important as a measure of the speed of growth once it has started.

An early spring mushroom is St George's mushroom (*Calocybe gambosa*). This edible mushroom takes its name from St George's Day, 23 April, by which time it should be visible in the fields and meadows if it is there at all. It is intermittent in its distribution, but the early appearance is useful in phenology as an indicator of rising temperatures. Both plant and fungus activity are equally affected by rising temperatures and day length. In the meadow and throughout the year, the cycles of activity are governed by these two factors, but the flexibility of onset is entirely due to differences in annual temperature. This variation is what is measured in studies of phenology, which mostly deal with plants as animals are intrinsically unpredictable. One such unpredictable animal is the mole (*Talpa europaea*). These mate in March and April, depending apparently upon their inclination. Most likely it is availability of food that determines the exact date that the mole hills return, which in itself is temperature dependent. Although they are mainly subterranean, moles can occasionally be seen above ground, where their strange gait marks them out from other small mammals. Moles are good to have around but the mole hills, heaves, can cause problems with our cutter by jamming and blunting the blade when they are hidden in the long vegetation and we cannot avoid them. Somehow this does not seem to matter when put against the alternative of a mole catcher. We are there for the benefit of the meadow, the meadow is not there for our benefit, so we should respect all the inhabitants. If we gain pleasure and knowledge from the meadow, so much the better, but we always need to be mindful that what is present is fulfilling a purpose in the ecology and removing one element will have a disruptive effect that might not be foreseen until it is too late to rectify. So no mole catcher, and the money we save we spend on repairs to our grass cutter.

During March the hedges become festooned with the flowers of blackthorn or sloe (*Prunus spinosa*). In this genus the sloe is quite an unprepossessing fruit as it shares its taxon with plums, cherries, peaches and almonds. You can see that while most of them have edible flesh and inedible seed, it is the other way around for almonds. We plant blackthorn in the large meadow hedge line as food supply and cover, but are aware that this may cause us trouble later as it was the least favourite of the traditional hedgers and ditchers. The simple reason for this is that the thorns are numerous, sharp and inclined to leave their ends in unprotected skin. Blackthorn is insect pollinated, so any early insects are welcome to visit the flowers, which includes some of the early bumblebees. Even so, frosts (Figure 5.1) can bring such early activity to a temporary stop.

Rabbits (*Oryctolagus cuniculus*) are starting to make themselves at home in the large meadow as the spring progresses. During these early months of the year they are clearly visible and consequently difficult to get close to. As the flowers and grass start to grow in profusion the rabbits are easier to approach, but only because they think

Figure 5.1. *Long shadows of early morning across a frosted meadow.*

they are hiding. When they do get up and run their passage can be followed by the swaying of the vegetation as they run through it.

The stunning snake's-head fritillary (*Fritillaria meleagris*) is the first plant to flower in spring in the small meadow (Figure 5.2) and while the number in flower can fluctuate dramatically from year to year, the timing is always pretty consistent: early April just before the cowslips.

Timing is critical for pollination as all of the plants must flower around the same time if they are going to be able to exchange pollen. Fritillaries, like other early spring bulbs, such as bluebells and daffodils, depend on making the most of the warmth and sunlight of late spring before the meadow's summer perennials grow up and take their light. Their strategy is to power very rapid early spring growth and flowering from the reserves they stored away at the end of the previous season, after which they need to lie dormant through the summer, ready in the late winter for the big push. The evidence suggests that temperature is the major factor controlling dormancy. Higher soil temperature and lower soil moisture forces the bulbs into dormancy in early summer and a period of lower soil temperature is needed to break dormancy. Commercial growers keep bulbs at 5°C for thirteen to seventeen weeks to do this and thus ensure predictable and uniform flowering of pot-grown fritillaries for sale. In nature the bulbs start growing in the autumn, the shoot slowly grows up towards the soil surface, reaching it sometime early in the winter. Here it stays until, probably triggered by both temperature and day length, it starts fast above-ground shoot growth in mid-late February.

The fluctuation in the number of fritillaries that flower every year is largely explained by their rather tortuous life history. Adults do not flower until their bulb is big enough, at which point the bulb is completely consumed to produce the plant. So every year the plant must grow a new bulb, together with seed, if it has flowered. Also, bulbs can split off bulblets from their bases. Bulb, seed and bulblet all make claims on the reserves the plant builds up while it is growing. If the season is poor or last year's bulb was only big enough for a small plant, the new bulb might not be big enough to allow the plant to flower. In nature it takes many years to go from seedling to flowering plant and survival, particularly in the early years, can be poor. In the year when the seed germinates, the plant is no more than a single, small, filamentous seed-leaf about the same size as a cat's whisker. There follows years as a juvenile, with just a single true leaf, a sub-adult, with two or three leaves, a vegetative adult, with four to eight leaves, before finally the bulb is big enough, at 12–20mm, to produce a flowering plant, also with four to eight leaves. This whole cycle can take as much as eight years. If you plant fritillaries as seeds in your meadow, you need plenty of patience. At any stage a plant can revert if it has a bad year or the adults can simply remain dormant underground resting. As long as there are enough plants at different stages in your meadow, you should be able to see some of these lovely flowers every year.

Figure 5.2. *Snake's-head fritillary on 11 April in the small meadow.*

A meadow pond, probably an old livestock pond, in one corner of the large meadow is a great delight and will spring to life late in the winter with the activities of common frogs (*Rana temporaria*) and smooth newts (*Lissotriton vulgaris*) as they spawn. By the time spring arrives, any suitable pond will have moved from spawn to tadpoles, gathered at the edge of the pond like a tidemark. In dry areas during the spring, the gorse, *Ulex europaeus*, flowers. It starts early and just runs on through the summer, giving cover for the more adventurous birds and animals. As the gorse grows, a clear area develops underneath the plants where lower branches have disappeared and there is neither light nor water to support other vegetation. This clear area is exploited by the rabbits and foxes (*Vulpes vulpes*) as refuge during the day, and probably muntjacs (*Muntiacus reevesi*) as well, but I suspect they stay clear of each other. Our rabbits tend to be open-ground animals rather than tunnellers, although they do dig. We think this is because the soil is too loose and shallow in the open to physically support a warren. Any rabbit holes we have tend to be in the field boundary, among the roots of the hawthorn (*Crataegus monogyna*) and other hedging species.

It is 31 March. Looking closely I can see tiny seedlings of yellow rattle (*Rhinanthus minor*) all across the small meadow (Figure 5.3). Yellow rattle is an annual plant and a partial, or hemi, parasite. It needs to get going early to thrive. Although it is green and produces its own food by photosynthesis, it needs to attach itself to surrounding plants to get a good supply of water and nutrients, and a substantial amount of carbon in the form of sugars as well. The seedling's roots grow down into the surrounding soil and when they encounter the roots of other plants they break into them and grow through to the centre, where they connect to the host's water-carrying vessels. These special structures produced by the yellow rattle are called haustoria.

Plants have two plumbing systems, one going downwards towards the roots carrying sugars made by photosynthesis in the leaves and the other going upwards towards the leaves carrying water sucked in by the roots. It is the upward system of plumbing, called the xylem, that yellow rattle taps into with its haustoria. The xylem also carries nutrients like nitrogen and potassium taken in from the surrounding soils, and amino acids, certain sugars and various other compounds produced by the plant's metabolism. The water flows upwards because the plant creates a potential difference, a kind of suction force, by keeping the concentration of soluble substances in the cells of the leaves higher than in the cells of the roots. Water, of course, is an essential resource for plants. Without it the leaves and young shoots will wilt and, critically, photosynthesis will stop working. Most plants conserve water when they do not need it by closing the pores in their leaves. Not yellow rattle, it is profligate. It keeps its pores open all of time and accumulates sugar alcohols in its leaves. These are potent in creating a suction force. In this way yellow rattle steals a constant flow of water, and all of the goodies dissolved in it, from its host, even at night or times of water stress.

Figure 5.3. *Yellow rattle in full flower at the end of May. It is a popular source of nectar for the common carder bumblebee (**Bombus pascuorum**), one of the longer-tongued bumblebees.*

The battle between yellow rattle and host is quite delicately balanced. Often hosts fight back. Some are more resistant to root break-in than others, some block off the haustoria once they have been formed and some are less affected even when the haustoria are fully functional. It is not just water and nutrients that the yellow rattle wants to sequester, the rattle must fight its host for light as well. The closer it grows to its host the bigger the water source and the more effective are its haustoria, because the roots and their xylem vessels are much bigger closer to the stem. Conversely, the closer it grows to its host the more shaded it will be and the less light it will have for photosynthesis – a yellow rattle attached to a host but made to grow in the dark will die. This means that the early days in its life are very critical. It does not have a very fine root system and so it is not very efficient at water and nutrient uptake until it attaches, and the seedling takes about three weeks to do this. Having a big seed with lots of food reserves and germinating early helps a lot here, but if the surrounding vegetation grows up before it can attach, a seedling is in danger of being shaded out or not being able to grow strongly enough to produce flowers or seed. Yellow rattle is an annual plant and its seeds only remain viable for one winter. This is why yellow rattle is not useful in meadows growing on high-fertility soils. Here the other plants are too vigorous and out-compete the seedling rattles for light, so little or no seed is produced and it gradually dies out.

Figure 5.4. *Primroses brighten up the spring as they come into flower in the shelter of hedges.*

When yellow rattle does grow well in a meadow its effect goes far beyond the first-order reduction in vigour of its hosts, because in doing this it also changes the structure of the sward and increases the diversity of plant species in the community. In turn, those changes will attract new insects and arthropods, both herbivores and the herbivores' predators. Yellow rattle is known to affect things underground as well, such as nutrient cycling and microbial communities, and these too will have implications for diversity. It truly is an ecosystem engineer.

As March moves into April the days are long enough and the ground warm enough for the grass to start growing in earnest. Also appearing in March and April are the two harbingers of sunny springtime, primroses (*Primula vulgaris*) (Figure 5.4) and cowslips (*Primula veris*) (Figure 5.5).

These two closely related flowers appear at about the same time, with cowslips favouring the open full sun of the meadow and the primroses staying close to the partial shade of hedges and in the large meadow the scrubby area, which contains hawthorn and gorse.

The stiff and rather untidy-looking yellow-green spikes of sweet vernal grass (*Anthoxanthum odoratum*) (Figure 5.6) are just about the first grass flowers to be seen in meadows across the country. It is sweet vernal grass that gives new-mown hay

Figure 5.5. *Cowslips flower early in the spring and like the open aspect of the large meadow.*

Figure 5.6. *Flower spikes of sweet vernal grass with meadow buttercup and oxeye daisy (***Leucanthemum vulgare***).*

its characteristic smell. The plant is packed with a biochemical compound called coumarin that, by harvest time, can comprise as much as 2.5% of the leaf dry weight, which is a huge amount for a secondary metabolite. Coumarin's taste, described as having a hint of vanilla, made its stalks the grass of choice for chewing while working the fields. As coumarin is also an appetite suppressor, this may also be a reason for chewing it mid-morning when breakfast is past and lunch a long way off.

Sweet vernal grass does not accumulate coumarin so that we can enjoy the smell of the harvest. Coumarin is an allelopathic compound, a chemical produced by a plant to affect the growth of surrounding plants or animals. It is readily washed out of the leaves and into the soil by rain, and it is also exuded directly into the soil by the roots, from where it moves, dissolved in water, to be taken up by the roots of other plants. Coumarin has been found to delay the germination of seeds of other species that do not contain coumarin themselves, and speed up germination of those that do. It also inhibits the root growth of other plants. Its effectiveness depends on soil type, the presence of microbes that can break it down before it reaches the other plants and the other plants' defences. Yet, and counter-intuitively, when sweet vernal grass is grown in a mixture with other species, each species does better than would be expected from their performance when they are grown separately. This is a well-established phenomenon and why diverse meadows are better at carbon storage than monocultures, both above ground and below.

Sweet vernal grass is so widespread because it produces masses of seed; in ideal conditions a single plant can produce up to 30,000, although in nature it is typically much less but still a considerable amount. The spikelet with its barbed awns, one bent and one straight, and hairy seed coat could easily become entangled in fur, feathers or clothing to aid distribution. Interestingly, the bent awn also has a trick up its sleeve. At the bend there is a special section of spiral, hygroscopic fibres. As these wet (or dry) the spiral reverses direction and the bend in the awn flips from one side to the other. This has the effect of making the seed move – it can even flick it for several centimetres – and, on soil, it means it could wriggle into cracks, effectively planting itself. Dispersal, then, is well catered for but its genetic plasticity is more important for its tolerance of a wide range of soils. In the long-running Park Grass Experiment at Rothamsted, where the only difference between adjacent plots has been their treatment with fertiliser and lime, some sweet vernal grass ecotypes have emerged in less than sixty-five years.

Primroses are an early treat for bumblebees and another insect that turns up from time to time, the dark-edged bee fly (*Bombylius major*). This small fly looks and behaves like a ginger bumblebee and can often be seen around the early flowers of primroses (Figure 5.7).

Dark-edged bee flies have an interesting life cycle, starting when they lay eggs in the vicinity of solitary bee nests. The fly finds a nest and can be seen to flick its eggs

Figure 5.7. *Dark-edged bee fly on primroses in the large meadow in spring.*

towards the nest hole. Once hatched, the larva makes its way to the nest, where it eats the contents of the cells and even the bee larva themselves. One such solitary bee that hosts the bee fly is the tawny mining bee (*Andrena fulva*) (Figure 5.8), which we have in the large meadow, where the bees make nests in the sandy soil that is ideally suited to their mining activity.

While the low-growing primroses nestle quietly in the mottled shade of larger plants, cowslips live in the open, and this can be a problem for them. Our muntjac deer seem to be partial to small meadow flowers, such as cowslips. The sign that they have received the attention of the deer is the removal of the flower, as though neatly snipped by a pair of scissors, as shown in Figure 5.9.

This method of just eating the flower is not confined to cowslips; our orchids suffer the same treatment, with the lovely pinky-purple flower spikes of common spotted orchids (*Dactylorhiza fuchsii*) being snipped off just below the flower. Precisely why the flowers are eaten

Figure 5.8. *Female tawny mining bee resting in the sun.*

Figure 5.9. *The snipped stems of cowslips in the large meadow, the sure sign of deer activity.*

but not the stems or leaves remains unknown, but we can guess that the deer like the sweet nectar associated with the open flowers.

Although hawthorn has another name 'may', denoting its traditional month of flowering in the UK, it is flowering earlier, so by April we can find it adorning the large meadow's hedges (Figure 5.10). The beautiful white flowers, although small, can completely cover the tree. Later in the year these will produce the haws that feed territorial thrushes and clumsy wood pigeons (*Columba palumbus*). By mid-April our few bluebells (*Hyacinthoides non-scripta*) are in flower, tucked under the trees at the top of the field. These are often considered shade plants, but in truth they are shade avoiders, growing and flowering in the early months of the year to gain access to the sunshine before the woodland canopy opens fully and shades the woodland floor.

During the spring the aerial acrobats arrive. Of all the avian visitors from the south, it is the swift (*Apus apus*) that outperforms them all. Their mating flights and banshee calls are quite amazing, but even though they are one of our most agile fliers, they can be caught by the hobby (*Falco subbuteo*). This bird of prey lends its name to the table top football game Subbuteo. The story is told that the game's inventor, Peter Adolph, originally tried to trademark 'hobby' for the game, but was told this was not possible due to common usage, so he hit on the

Figure 5.10. *In April hawthorn adorns the hedge lines of our fields, interspersed with the oak trees just coming into leaf with the yellow blush of their first leaves and their flowers.*

ornithological solution of using the latinised form. The hobby may be able to catch a swift for dinner, but it is no easy task. While it is larger and more powerful than the swift, the swift is more agile due to the construction of the wing. The swift wing seems to share a common evolutionary origin with hummingbirds. With a short humerus and greater proportion of primary wing feathers than normal, speed and manoeuvrability come as second nature to swifts.

It is in the spring months while the meadow wakes up, that most graceful of all roses, the dog rose (*Rosa canina*), comes into flower along the boundaries of the large meadow and in the scrub area (Figure 5.11). Although lovely to look at, they make for an almost impenetrable barrier to human excursions into our scrub, protecting the wildlife with living barbed wire.

A meadow can look like an ordinary piece of pasture in early spring, but this is a trap for the unobservant. While the plants are small, their variety can easily be overlooked. This is because very few have distinctive leaves when they are small. Some do, however, like the common spotted orchid, which has leaves so distinctively marked in purple that the plant is a striking meadow plant as soon as it starts growing (Figure 5.12).

Figure 5.11. *The dog roses that grow in the field boundaries and scrub area of the large meadow flower in the spring and summer.*

Many other species will only become apparent when they flower, and then they will mostly disappear back into the green background as soon as the flowers go over and lose their colour. Of course, they are still there, setting seed and growing vegetatively, adding to the diversity of the meadow but in a quiet and unnoticed way. These plants are like individuals lost in the congestion of a football crowd of vegetation; they may seem individually insignificant, but they are the plants that make up a happy meadow.

Orchids are the star attraction of many a meadow, often headlining nature reserve notice boards. In the small meadow the southern marsh orchid (*Dactylorhiza praetermissa*) starts to flower in the last week of May (Figure 5.13). Its beauty is obvious enough. The simple, erect mid-green leaves are topped by a head of twenty to sixty flowers, coloured somewhere between purple and pink, and finely marked with darker spots and dashes. Like most orchids, it is quite capable of showing up as a fully formed flowering plant seemingly out of nowhere, with no sign of younger plants and the nearest seed source miles away.

The secret is in the dust-like seeds that are parasitic on fungi for their early growth. The seeds of southern marsh are less than 1mm long and 80% of the seed is air. The seed is made up of a thin seed coat one cell thick, formed like a net, and the tiny

Figure 5.12. *Common spotted orchids in the spring are a striking addition to the sward.*

Figure 5.13. *Southern marsh orchids start to flower at the end May in the small meadow. Some flowering yellow rattle can be seen in the background.*

embryo, a ball of just a few cells. Most plant seeds contain a store of food to see the embryo through germination and expansion of the first green leaves, but not orchids. The upshot is that orchid seeds can be carried for miles on turbulent winds but when they land they have to get food from some other organism to germinate. It is species of soil fungus that provide the food. The thin thread-like fungal hyphae grow into the orchid's cells and form coils that the orchid then digests. In this way the orchid can grow big enough to produce a small tuber and its first green leaf. Southern marsh orchids take a year or more to reach this stage. Nevertheless, with further input from the fungus plus the leaf's own photosynthesis, it usually grows a big enough tuber to be able to flower a year or two later. It is still not known whether the orchid is a full parasite or the relationship with the fungus is symbiotic. Certainly, the orchid is the major beneficiary and it seems to have all of the control. It only allows the fungus to grow into certain cells, it can change the fungus species it is using depending on circumstances and it can start and stop infection as necessary.

Many orchids trick pollinators into visiting their flowers with false promises. The well-known example of this is the sexual mimicry of the bee orchid (*Ophrys apifera*). Its flowers have the appearance of female solitary bees, duping the naive male bees, which have emerged before the real females, into trying to mate with them. In doing so the bee will pick up the pollen sac and pollinate the next flower it tries to mate with. In the UK, while the bee orchids flower happily, they are almost entirely self-pollinated because the natural pollinator cannot survive our winter weather. Southern marsh flowers are food deceptive in that they have the appearance of nectar-rich flowers but they provide no food at all. The flowers have 6mm spurs, where nectar would normally be found, and so are mostly visited by longer-tongued bumblebees. Like the bee orchid, the southern marsh seems to be relying on fooling young naive bees, those that have not yet learnt the flowers are empty. It is not clear what attracts the bees to the orchid; it may be the large number of flowers in the spike, the purplish-pink colouration or perhaps a scent, although the flowers appear scentless to us. Bees learn which flowers do not have nectar more slowly than they learn those that do but when they do learn they visit fewer of the flowers on a spike where the flowers have no nectar. In this way food deceit may encourage out-crossing as well as saving the cost of making nectar. There are disadvantages, too. Food-deceptive orchids get far fewer visitors than food-rewarding orchids and they set less seed, although there is always plenty on the southern marsh orchids in the small meadow.

It is during the spring that an unexpected plant puts in an appearance, oak saplings. Almost like magic, they arrive a long way from the oak trees in the hedge line, but they are all yearlings and will be cut down with the hay. In the large meadow we believe the magic ingredient is the magpie (*Pica pica*). These constantly active and chattering birds have become more and more common over the last forty years, to such an extent that we often have a flock of these birds. The more pedantic will prefer the collective noun of a gulp of magpies, a mischief of magpies, or a conventicle of magpies. Although all of these have been used at one time or another, the one thing they all have in common is an element of the ill-disciplined or unruly, which pretty well sums up magpie behaviour. Lined up on the fence, they seem to shout at each other and any passing animal, including me. Every year the magpies forget about a few of the acorns they buried and these readily germinate. It is no wonder that oak scrub can form on an unmanaged meadow plot very quickly.

By May the meadow buttercup *(Ranunculus acris)* is in full flower, its season running from April to October. This is generally avoided by grazing animals as it contains an unstable glucoside that is enzymatically split if the plant is damaged to produce glucose and protoamenonin, which is toxic, an aspect of the plant that is reflected in the name *acris*. So while the meadow is in full flower the meadow buttercup produces a wonderful show of dancing yellow flowers, left uneaten by grazing livestock. When the hay is cut and dried, this toxic compound is further broken down so that it is rendered harmless and makes a happy addition to the winter fodder.

Other yellow flowers that can feature in large numbers in a meadow are the dandelions (*Taraxacum*) and their lookalikes, certain members of the hawkbit (*Leontodon/Scorzoneroides*), hawksbeard (*Crepis*), hawkweed (*Hieracium*) and cat's-ear (*Hypochaeris*) genera. Dandelions and hawkweeds are unusual in that they contain what are termed apomictic species. These are plants that produce seed without pollination. In Britain all hawkweeds and almost all dandelions are apomictic. The evolutionary process that created them means that there are lots of very similar-looking species, sometimes called micro species. In fact we have about 240 species of dandelion in Britain. Plants grown from their seeds are in every sense clones of the adult from which they came. This is the same as plants grown from runners, except that in the case of these producers of airborne seeds, a single seed can hop the hedgerow and spread into a nearby field to start a colony. The similarity of the species is a headache for the botanist trying to make a correct identification and most do not try, simply referring to them all as *Taraxacum* agg. Of course, you can just enjoy them for what they are – flowers shining from spring to autumn.

Spring is the time that the butterflies start to make an appearance, warm early spring days coax out the hibernating small tortoiseshells (*Aglais urticae*), which will disappear back into their hiding places if the weather turns cold again. These are among our longest-living butterflies, able to survive for several years if they successfully hibernate through consecutive winters. Later on the new butterflies emerge from overwintering pupae. These can be attached to hard surfaces, such as in the large white (*Pieris brassicae*), green-veined white (*Pieris napi*) and small white (*Pieris rapae*) butterflies, or at ground level in the case of the marbled white (*Melanargia galathea*). The last, although called marbled white, is actually a 'brown' and is not closely related to the whites at all.

It is 11 April and orange-tips (*Anthocharis cardamines*) are out and about, the first butterflies of the year to visit the small meadow (Figure 5.14). Orange-tips do not hibernate, so these individuals must be newly emerged from a pupae. The butterfly with the orange tips to its upper forewings is the male. The female does not have the orange wing tips and from above can be confused with a small white or a green-veined white, which start flying around the same time. Underneath, however, both sexes have the most beautiful mottled green rear wing that, when they are at rest, makes them both easy to identify and difficult to see. The green colour is a visual illusion; the scales that make it are actually black and yellow. Scales are dead material produced by the butterfly's skin cells. Each cell produces one scale made from a stack of layers so thin that they interfere with light to make the colour. One of the most interesting and surprising aspects of animal colours is that they have no blue pigments; all those lovely blues that you see on butterflies and beetles are structural colours created by the same process as the green of orange-tip butterflies.

Male orange-tips are more likely to be seen, partly because they stand out so clearly with their orange-tipped wings and partly because they spend much longer on the wing than females. The males spend most of their time in the air patrolling,

Figure 5.14. *A female orange-tip butterfly sitting on lady's smock, her larvae's food plant. She is probably checking if it is good enough for one of her eggs.*

looking for females to mate with; while females spend most of their time among vegetation laying their eggs. This difference in activity is thought to explain the colour dimorphism – the male, which is most visible to predators, being on the wing so much, has orange wing tips to warn those predators that it is unpleasant to eat as it is full of mustard oils accumulated from the food plants consumed during the larval stage. The females are much more cryptic. Their lack of orange and the superb camouflage offered by the mottled underwing help to hide them from predators among the vegetation. Those mustard oils, chemically glucosinolates, are, ironically, produced by the host plant as protection against being eaten. Glucosinolates are deadly to some butterflies but the whites (family *Pieridae*) have wrought an evolutionary battle with their cabbage family food plants so that not only are they able to tolerate the glucosinolates, but they have even turned them to their advantage in making the larvae and adults unpalatable to predators. Ironically, the glucosinolates may be the very chemicals that attract the female to lay her eggs on the plant.

Orange-tips' usual habitats of damp meadows and hedgerows reflect the habitats of the preferred food plants of the larvae, lady's smock (*Cardamine pratensis*) in meadows and garlic mustard (*Alliaria petiolata*) in hedgerows. The adults sip nectar from these and a wide range of other spring flowers, but it is garlic mustard and lady's smock where the female lays her eggs. These are laid singly, one per plant, because the larvae are cannibalistic and the first to emerge from the egg will eat any other eggs in the proximity. It seems that she can detect the presence of another egg on the plant, and also determine that it is a suitable host species by tasting it with her feet. The egg takes a week or two to hatch and the tiny caterpillar starts eating immediately, first its own eggshell, then any other eggs in the vicinity and then the seed pods of its host. By July the caterpillar is big enough to spin itself into a cocoon, which is attached to twigs of more substantial plants. Here it spends most of its life – the nine months or so before emerging the following April.

The small meadow is nothing if not damp and lady's smock has found its own way into it. As yet, there are only a few plants, and the visiting orange-tips probably grew up elsewhere, but no doubt it would have been full of lady's smock when it was part of a much bigger traditional meadow. The large meadow, on the other hand, is sandy and dry. Neither lady's smock nor garlic mustard grow in it and orange-tips are only seen as transitory visitors.

Swallows (*Hirundo rustica*) patrol the large meadow almost at ground level, scooping up the insects that are lifted from the ground by rising thermals blowing up the slope. Our soil is so light that it is already starting to dry out. Land with more organic matter in the soil will have a greater water-carrying capacity and will still be untroubled by lack of rain. We have neither drainage ditches nor winter ponds in field corners as the ground drains so quickly through the soil. The reason we have such light soil is that it is made from weathered sand dunes, dunes that were themselves originally fossilised into solid blocks of rock. Even though it looks very much like the fossil-bearing sandstone of other parts of the world, we have no fossils. Their stone is alluvial, while ours was blown into shape before being solidified.

By the end of May all the plants of the meadow and surrounding hedgerows are in full leaf, and many have started to flower. It is easy to say all foliage is green, but there are as many shades and tones of green as there are plants, especially in the spring. It is in many ways odd that we only have one word for green when it is the most variable of natural shades, the product of unused light in photosynthesis.

When the hawthorn is over the elderberry (*Sambucus nigra*) has come into flower. Although a common country plant, it makes for poor hedging as the stems snap far too easily for it to be layered. As spring moves into summer, temperatures rise and while the official changeover takes place on 20 or 21 June, the summer solstice, the plants and animals of our meadows pay no attention to man-made calendars but carry on eating and breeding to ensure their survival.

CHAPTER 6

Meadows in summer

Summer comes in with no signs of change from spring, a flawless transition of seasons. That is what you should expect, considering the way the seasons are constructed. Astronomically, summer is said to start on 21 June in the Northern Hemisphere and 22 December in the Southern. With the earth permanently cranked over at about 23.4° it is these dates at which the Northern or Southern Hemispheres are at maximum direct exposure to the sun, being most tilted towards the sun. This is despite the orbit around the sun being elliptical, with a difference of 5 million km between the long axis and the short axis, and the earth being nearest to the sun during the southern summer and furthest during the northern summer. Notwithstanding the complexity of celestial orbits, summer is most easily defined as the warmest three months of the year, running as it does from 21 June to 23 September. This range of dates inevitably includes part of the year that sees one of the most important annual activities in the meadow, which we normally referred to as the autumn cut. In some hot and dry years this cutting and clearing has been finished before the end of summer, but generally I like to let the flowers completely go over and seed before starting the cut.

Bird's-foot trefoil (*Lotus corniculatus*) is one of the slower plants to start flowering, at least in the small meadow (Figure 6.1). It is another of the meadow wildflowers that is very widespread and tolerant of a range of environments. Nevertheless, it has a preference for drier soils just on the acid side of neutral, which is perhaps why sandy soils, like those of the large meadow, suit it while it struggles a bit on the wet, heavy soil of the small meadow. There are two aspects of its physiology that help it to grow in such a wide range of soils. Like most of the pea family, it can form a symbiotic relationship with bacteria to capture nitrogen from the air and it has an arsenal of chemical defences against herbivores.

Nitrogen is probably the most important element for plant growth after carbon. Although 78% of the atmosphere is nitrogen, it is not directly available to plants. Symbiotic bacteria incorporate nitrogen gas into ammonia, a form of nitrogen that the plant can work with. The plant provides sugars to power this conversion, which uses a lot of energy. This is because the two nitrogen atoms in a molecule of nitrogen gas are very tightly bonded together and they must be split apart. In

Figure 6.1. *Bird's-foot trefoil in the meadow of a local nature reserve with the day-flying latticed heath moth* (**Chiasmia clathrata**) *sipping nectar.*

peas 30% of the carbon assimilated by the plant during photosynthesis is provided to the nitrogen-fixing nodules as sugars but then 15% is returned in the form of amino acids. The plants do not have to incur this cost if they are already growing in a nitrogen-rich environment, so bird's-foot trefoil does not grow nodules if it is fed with nitrogen fertiliser. In environments where nitrogen is in short supply the plant attracts suitable nitrogen-fixing bacteria by releasing a signal chemical into the soil surrounding its roots. In the huge cocktail of free living bacteria that live around the roots, species such as *Rhizobia* will detect the plant's signal and respond by producing their own signal chemical. So too will prospective pathogenic bacteria that have read the plant's signal. If a bacterium's signal chemical is recognised by the plant as coming from *Rhizobia*, it starts to grow a nodule and allows the bacterium to infect it. Once in the nodule the bacterium is taken into a cell and surrounded by a plant membrane so that it becomes very like any other organelle. The bacterium makes changes to its cell surface and its metabolism, becoming better adapted to life within a cell dedicated to nitrogen fixation. If the signalling exchange is not quite right the plant's defence systems can be triggered and no nodules are produced. In this way the plant can protect itself against pathogenic bacteria and select the best nitrogen fixers.

Bird's-foot trefoil has some clever chemical tricks up its sleeve for defence against herbivores as well. It makes two types of compound intended to stop it being eaten: tannins, which can cause digestion problems in both insects and mammals, and cyanogenic glycosides, which release cyanide when the plant cells are crushed. The cyanide is rarely toxic but is distasteful enough to put off generalist feeders that are happy to move on to other species rather than continue eating bird's-foot trefoil. The plant has a good deal of control as to which defence to use, when to use it, and where to use it. For example, it is more likely to deploy them in young leaves because they are more efficient at photosynthesis and their loss of greater significance to the plant. It may also divert the resources used for defence compounds to more important parts like seeds. Herbivores, of course, have been co-evolving with bird's-foot trefoil and have been more or less successful in creating countermeasures, either to destroy the defence compounds or to overcome their harmful effects. Specialist herbivores that feed on only one or a very few plants have, by definition, been very successful at this. The common blue butterfly (*Polyommatus icarus*) is one such. Its larvae produce an enzyme that detoxifies cyanide, and they quite happily feed on bird's-foot trefoil as their main food plant. They have also overcome the effect of tannins on their digestion because bird's-foot trefoil that is producing more tannins than cyanogenic glycosides is preferred to those producing more cyanogenic glycosides than tannins.

The dawn chorus becomes less of a feature as the summer moves on and parent birds spend less time proclaiming territory and more time foraging for food for their continuously hungry broods. On the other hand, while bird song diminishes, the insect chorus increases, becoming a perfect indicator of sunshine and warmth; the hotter and brighter it gets, the louder they become. While this is the time to enjoy the meadow, it is also time for careful use of a sweep net. Keeping clear of the flowers in the large meadow as much as I can so that I don't sweep up the more delicate meadow residents, such as butterflies and bees, sweeping the nettles (*Urtica dioica*) and grasses can produce some interesting creatures. Although most of the sweeps bring up large quantities of insects, during the summer the majority are bugs, most notably *Nabis ferus*, which eats other insects and caterpillars. The adults overwinter to emerge in the spring and lay their eggs. Once hatched the nymphs eat other insects, so by August they are fully winged adults. Another predatory bug that appears in the summer sweep net in large numbers is the smaller black and white species *Anthocoris nemoralis*. This particular insect has the unenviable reputation of being a bit of a biter. If one gets on your skin it will wander about a bit before testing the ground it is on for edibility, which it does by using its piercing mouthparts. These are normally used to pierce the skin of aphids and small insect nymphs, which it then sucks the juice out of.

More interesting finds when sweeping are large but relatively common crickets and grasshoppers. The most common species in the large meadow is the common green grasshopper (*Omocestus viridulus*). Like the bugs that turn up in the net, they are

Figure 6.2. *A female speckled bush cricket. The sickle-shaped ovipositor is used to lay eggs in the bark of trees.*

hemimetabolous, that is they hatch from the egg, more or less as miniature versions of the adult. This contrasts with the holometabolous species such as butterflies and beetles where there are distinct stages unlike each other – egg, larva, pupae, adult. While common green grasshoppers may be the most common grasshopper we find, the occasional unusual species does turn up from time to time. One that did surprise me was the speckled bush cricket (*Leptophyes punctatissima*) (Figure 6.2). This was unexpected because the eggs are laid in the bark of trees and although we do have a few, there are not a lot of them, but obviously enough to maintain a population. The nymphs of speckled bush crickets feed on our brambles (*Rubus fruticosus* agg.), of which we do have a considerable amount.

Another unusual and pleasing find lurking in the bottom of the sweep net has been Roesel's bush cricket (*Metrioptera roeselii*). These very active insects proved difficult to photograph as they are permanently restless as adults, so the photograph (Figure 6.3a) was taken with my head in the net.

Roesel's bush cricket normally has short wings as an adult, but there is a long-winged form that we do not seem to have. The eggs are laid in plant stems, the nymphs emerging in May and June. After several moults the adults can be seen around the end of July, often right into October if the weather holds. An unusual

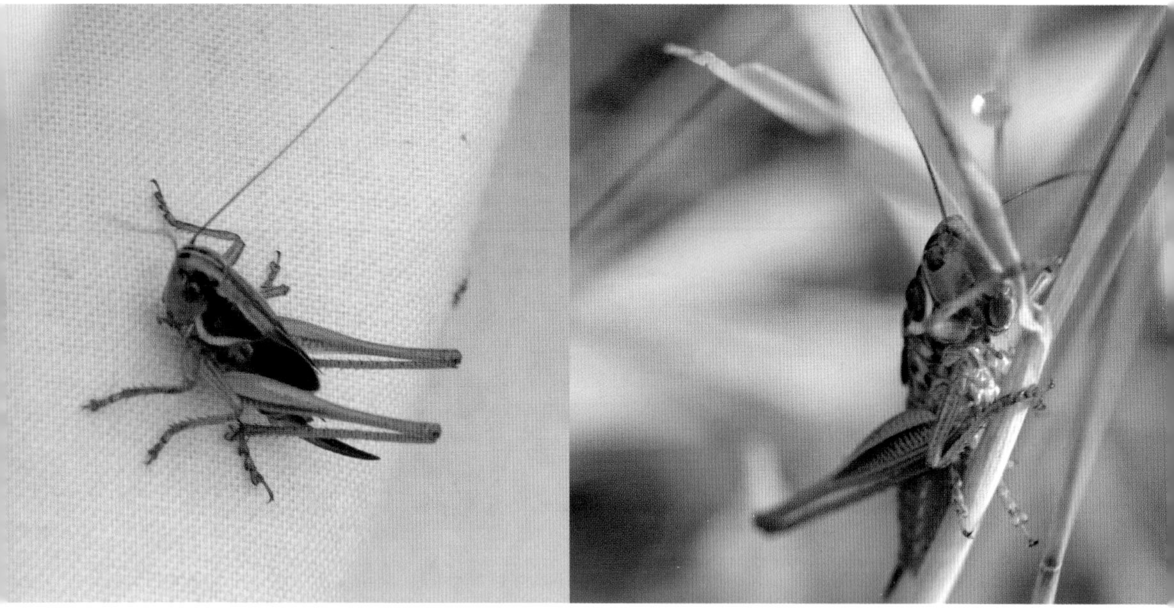

Figure 6.3. *a) Female Roesel's bush cricket (left). The ovipositor is used to cut the plant stems that she will lay her eggs in. b) Male Roesel's bush cricket (right).*

aspect of the distribution of this insect is that at the start of the twentieth century it was more or less confined to the coast from the Thames to the Humber. It has spent the last hundred years slowly extending its range both westwards and northwards, until we have it in the large meadow about as far from any coast as it is possible to be in Britain, and very welcome it is, too.

Dotted about the large meadow we have thistles and knapweeds, which from a distance look superficially the same, but become clearly distinguishable as you get closer. Most of our thistles are confined to the hedge line, where they were one of the few species, along with the nettles, that could cope with the damage done by the horses as they rubbed against the fence posts and over-grazed the area. The knapweeds are firm favourites with bees and butterflies. Some species, like red-tailed bumblebees (*Bombus lapidarius*), have been studied in considerable detail to demonstrate their importance to meadows (Figure 6.4).

Watch a bumblebee working a field of flowers and you will find that it tends only to visit flowers of one species of plant. It will fly by other flowers of a similar shape, colour and height. If there are several individuals of the same species flying at the same time, it is likely that they will all be foraging on flowers of that same species of plant as well. In contrast, if there is a different species of bee it is likely that it will be foraging on a different species of plant and this pattern is predictable for days at a time. In the small meadow the red-tailed's favourite is cat's-ear (*Hypochaeris radicata*). They swerve the oxeye daisies (*Leucanthemum vulgare*), same height, same shape, and meadow buttercups (*Ranunculus acris*), same height, same colour, and just fly from one cat's-ear flower to the next, visiting sixty to 100 flowers per trip. It is not that the red-taileds do not like the other flowers. Cat's-ear is one of those flowers that opens during the sunniest part of the day and in the small meadow at the height of summer this is about 8 a.m., earlier in the large meadow. Before this the red-taileds happily work the meadow buttercups collecting food.

The colony grows slowly through the summer. Red-tailed colonies can have up to 300 bees, and when it is large enough and has collected enough food it produces males and new queens. These are a big drain on the colony's nectar resources, because neither forage for the colony and the new queens consume a large amount of the colony's nectar store building up their body weight for the winter. Consequently, the appearance of males and queens signals the end of the colony.

Clearly, bumblebees are entirely dependent on flowers, so we might wonder just how much meadow is needed to support a bumblebee colony? Meadows are better than the same area of annual flowers because they produce much more food and they do it earlier in the year when the bee colonies are most actively growing. When in full flower, a square metre of good perennial meadow produces around 0.54g of

Figure 6.4. *Red-tailed bumblebees foraging on flowers of cat's ear. The female on the right has stored collected pollen on her leg baskets.*

pollen a day. To put this in context, it is known to take about 0.150g of pollen to produce a 0.122g honey bee (*Apis mellifera*) worker. By contrast, bumblebee workers vary enormously in size. The first brood can be tiny, but if we say an average red-tailed worker is twice the size of a honey bee worker and consequently requires twice as much pollen, we can estimate that a square metre of perennial meadow produces enough pollen to make nearly two red-tailed workers every day. With a bit of further extrapolation, in one month just 5.5 sq m will produce enough to grow a large red-tailed bumblebee colony of 300 bees.

Of course, the bees need to be as efficient as possible to collect all of this food and visiting flowers at random is not a good technique. It is more effective to be consistent by only visiting the most rewarding flower species over a period of days. Unlike honey bees, bumblebees do not communicate the location of food sources within the colony, but they do learn by watching other bumblebees of their species. They remember routes, and they can use colour, pattern, shape and scent as cues to spot the species they are currently collecting from. Since the colony lives for longer than the peak flowering of any wild flower, their chosen species will naturally change as time goes by. They can change their allegiance even during a single day if their preferred flower becomes either unavailable, because, say, it opens late or closes early, or less rewarding, because it produces most nectar in the morning or evening. It follows that the bumblebees depend on a mix of sequentially flowering species. Without them they would not survive, and equally without the bumblebees and other pollinators, the plant species would not survive and many of our crops would not grow.

It is no surprise that wood mice (*Apodemus sylvaticus*) (Figure 4.3) venture into the meadow during the spring and summer as the sward is tall enough to provide cover from predators and the meadow is packed with food in the form of seeds, these being a big part of the rodent's diet. Their average life span is just one year, with few surviving the winter. To make up for this they are prolific breeders, normally having four litters of five pups between February and October. If there is plenty of food and temperatures are not too low, they will even breed over the winter, with the newborns becoming sexually active at about two months. To maintain such a high rate of breeding they need to find a lot of food. In the summer, females, whose home ranges are smaller than males, can range over half a hectare, which is a huge area when you are so small, and one might reasonably ask how they navigate around it. On a human scale, imagine trying to find your way around 10 hectares of woodland, the size of more than twelve football pitches, with no paths and in the dark. There is good evidence that the wood mouse has an advantage in being able to detect the earth's magnetic field and uses it to orient itself. They have also been found to use objects as waymarkers when they are exploring, picking up and placing distinctive objects at the centre of areas of interest. They also seem to be familiar with their local area, wandering into any similar habitat in the general direction of home. The upshot is that a wood mouse knows its home range pretty well and can navigate more or less directly back to its burrow when released at random within it. To minimise risk from predators, wood mice prefer to collect larger food items. In woodland this often means choosing acorns of anything up to 60 or 70% of their body weight. In the small meadow garden I have watched them climbing, snipping off and carrying away whole seed heads of columbine (*Aquilegia vulgaris*).

By the time that summer is well under way flowers have become the residence, landing site, or feeding station for all manner of insects and spiders. It is at this time of year that the nursery web spider (*Pisaura mirabilis*) can be seen (Figure 6.5). This large spider takes its name from the web it spins, which is not to capture prey, but to protect the egg sac while the female stays on guard. These webs are really quite large and dense, bending over the supporting foliage whether it is grass or nettles. *Pisaura* is closely related to our largest spider, the great raft spider (*Dolomedes plantarius*), one of two large spiders in this genus that are referred to as raft spiders as they are capable of 'rafting' across still water by spreading their weight on outspread legs. Our nursery web spider is unusual in being one of very few spider species where the male will present a gift-wrapped insect to the female to entice her to mate. Such behaviour is very rare in spiders and as it is not a cannibalistic species it is certainly not an act

Figure 6.5. *Nursery web spider making its way across ragweed flowers.*

Figure 6.6. *Cinnabar moth caterpillar on ragwort. The black and yellow colouration is a warning to predators that this caterpillar is not edible.*

of self-preservation by the male. With a body length of 12–15mm, this is quite a hefty spider when fully grown and can be found forming nests among the nettles, or just generally wandering about. It is this wandering behaviour that makes it a regular find in the sweep net, especially when used among nettles.

Of course, the group of insects most often regarded as the epitome of summer are the butterflies and to a lesser extent the day-flying moths. Like many of the visitors and residents of the meadow, ragwort (*Jacobaea vulgaris*) provides nectar, pollen and food for their young. One of the best-known eaters of ragwort is the cinnabar moth (*Tyria jacobaeae*) caterpillar (Figure 6.6). This relationship is reflected in the name of the moth – before its recent change, ragwort's name was *Senecio jacobaea*.

Most of the butterflies that breed regularly in the meadow are common species, but that is not to say that they are not as lovely as the rarest transient visitor. The flash of blue that we see with the common blue shows us the flight of the male butterfly (Figure 6.7). The female is quite different and to a casual observer could almost be a different species, being very similar to the brown argus (*Aricia agestis*) (Figure 6.7).

As an adult, the common blue butterfly feeds on nectar, but the caterpillar, which is very small, reflecting the size of the butterfly, feeds on various legumes such as trefoils and clovers, and apparently even peas and beans. Pupation takes place among a few

Figure 6.7. *Left, underside of a common blue. Top right, the dusty blue of a male common blue bottom. Right, the upper-side of the wings of a brown argus, which is similar to the female common blue.*

threads of silk at the base of the food plant. Although the several blues that may be seen are difficult to separate from a distance, the common blue is the only species where the upper side of the male is completely blue and unmarked, while the underside has delightful orange markings (Figure 6.7a). Some of the caterpillars overwinter and resume feeding in the spring, so that by June the adults are starting to appear in the large meadow with large numbers skipping away from me as I move through the grass in July and August. The brown argus caterpillar feeds on various types of cranesbill, of which we have a lot, but what is strange is that this is generally regarded as a chalk hill species, not an acid grassland species such as we have. However, for as long as the food plant is available we hope the brown argus will stay; perhaps we shouldn't tell them they are in the wrong place.

There are other species that appear in considerable numbers in a hay meadow, clustered around the flowers. During the summer it is the dandelion-like flowers and those great favourites the knapweeds that attract most attention. Even though many of the dandelions have an asexual method of reproduction, as described in Chapter 5, they provide a welcome supply of nectar to various butterflies, like the marbled white (*Melanargia galathea*) in Figure 6.8.

On knapweeds all manner of insects can be found. Our knapweed is the common knapweed (*Centaurea nigra*), while further south on the chalky areas you are more

Figure 6.8. *Marbled white on the dandelion-like rough hawkbit* (Leontodon hispidus).

likely to come across the greater knapweed (*Centaurea scabiosa*). These two species can be confused if the knapweed is the rayed form – the rays look like feathery petals – but as far as the insects are concerned they are fast food, fly-through restaurants. The butterflies appreciate them as they flower throughout the summer, providing continuous refreshment to passing species like small skippers (*Thymelicus sylvestris*) (Figure 6.9) and peacock (*Nymphalis io*) butterflies that are large enough to completely cover the flower (Figure 6.10). The peacock feeds on the flowers but their caterpillars assist in controlling the nettles that grow around the meadow edge where previously grazed areas have been augmented with nitrogen from the horses' urine. Small skippers appear in large numbers at the height of the summer, their caterpillars having fed on grasses such as Yorkshire fog (*Holcus lanatus*) in the body of the meadow.

Another of the small butterflies that is difficult to mistake for any other is the small copper (*Lycaena phlaeas*) (Figure 6.11). It is not easy to identify with certainty the sex of the butterfly as it rushes past, busy finding food in the summer sun; you really need to see it settled to be able to do that. It varies in numbers from year to year, probably influenced by the availability of its preferred food plants, common sorrel (*Rumex acetosa*) and sheep's sorrel (*Rumex acetosella*). These are both types of dock and their

Figure 6.9. *Small skipper feeding on nectar from ragwort.*

Figure 6.10. *Peacocks that visit knapweed are one of the larger butterflies in the meadow.*

Figure 6.11. *A male small copper investigating ripening blackberries for exuded sugar as food.*

widespread distribution mirrors that of the small copper. This particular butterfly spends the entire summer in frantic activity, with three broods throughout the year, so they can be seen from late April right through to October.

Besides butterflies, beetles make much use of flowers for food as adults, irrespective of what the larva eats. Two examples of this are shown in Figure 6.12.

Rutpela maculata is a wood-boring beetle, so called because the larvae feed on timber. This species prefers dead and decaying wood, which as you can imagine, is not a very nutritious material. Living on low-nutrient food is reflected in the length of the life cycle, this being two to three years. Although in the large meadow we do not

Figure 6.12. **Rutpela maculata** *(left) and* **Cordylepherus viridis** (right). *As larva these beetles have quite different lives, but as adults they both make use of the flowers in the large meadow.*

have any of the trees normally used as food, like beech (*Fagus sylvatica*), ash (*Fraxinus excelsior*) and oaks, another species that we do have a number of and is used as a food supply for the larva is black pine (*Pinus nigra*). There is a line of mature examples across one edge of our meadow and these routinely drop branches during winter storms. This makes us very cautious about going up there and standing under the trees when the wind is blowing hard. We have never bothered moving these as we are aware that they provide food and shelter for various species, one of which is *Rutpela*. Once the adults of this species have emerged they make for the flowers, where they can feed on pollen. The other species in Figure 6.12, *Cordylepherus viridis*, is much smaller, but rather splendid when seen up close. This beetle also lays its eggs on fallen timber, generally wood that has already started to rot. The larva does not eat the wood but is predatory on other invertebrates smaller than itself. By contrast, the adult beetle generally eats pollen, although it is reported that it will eat very small invertebrates that it comes across while feeding on flowers.

Across many meadows, summer is the time when species of the aster family take centre stage. There is a long list of these that grow in meadows: thistles, knapweeds, ragworts, hawkweeds, hawkbits, dandelions and daisies, and cat's-ear is one that is commonly found. Like all members of the family, its flower is made up of many tiny flowers, called florets, closely aggregated into a single head. The flowers of their very distant ancestor will have been individually stalked and in clusters – perhaps in an umbel, like elderberry (*Sambucus nigra*), or a panicle, like meadowsweet (*Filipendula ulmaria*), or a spike, like agrimony (*Agrimonia eupatoria*). Over the aeons, all of the stalks in the ancestor's flower cluster gradually shortened to nothing and the flowers joined together into a compound flower head. The five petals of the original flowers fused into a tube, sometimes with a strap-shaped, petal-like ray to one side of the tube. In thistles the florets are all tubular, in oxeye daisy the florets around the outside of the flower have rays, giving the typical daisy appearance of a yellow centre with a fringe of white petals, and in cat's-ear and dandelions all of the florets have rays. The sepals that would normally be the flower bud coverings became a ring of hairs and the leaves that were beneath each of the flowers became the new bud coverings.

It is fascinating to mark a single cat's-ear flower and watch as it blooms and turns to seed because you can see how superbly this complicated structure has been adapted for cross-pollination and seed dispersal (Figure 6.13). The florets are arranged in a spiral. On the first day of flowering only the outer ring of florets open, the rays lying flat while the business end of the flower, the anthers and stigma, are held vertically. The rays of the unopened florets are grouped together in a central vertical column. This gives bees a landing platform on the open rays that they can walk around while collecting nectar and pollen from the floret tubes. In the late afternoon, when the sun is far from overhead or when the flowers have dipped into shade, they will close up for the day. The following day the next outermost unopened ring of florets open ready for pollination, and so it continues every day until all six or seven rings are pollinated. Back in the late 1940s Mary Percival watched in great detail as cat's-ear flowers opened and honey bees pollinated them. She found that the flowers' opening is triggered by bright sunshine and on rainy days the flowers may not open at all – the same conditions that determine whether bees leave the hive to forage. Also, since pollen is gradually removed from the florets as the day progresses, she found bees have to visit more and more flowers to collect a full load of pollen, from about twenty early on to 150 later in the day. A full pollen load is about 0.01g, the weight of half a grain of rice.

Once the whole spiral of florets has been pollinated, the flower closes for about three weeks to protect the developing seeds. As the seed grows, so do the hairs that were once the sepals of the floret. In cat's-ear these grow into the seed's parachute and, when the base of the flower eventually dries out and curls back on itself almost into a ball, the parachutes open and form the characteristic dandelion clock. A stiff breeze can then carry the seeds off to distant meadows. Actually, the cat's-ear parachute is pretty ragged and in still air the seed-and-parachute combo falls a metre in only a little over three and a half seconds, which is still quite slow compared with the fraction of a second it takes if you remove the parachute and drop just the seed from a metre above ground. It is interesting to do the same experiment outdoors. Try dropping a seed with its parachute attached from the height of the average open clock. Even with no perceptible breeze the seed will drift perhaps for 20cm; with a stronger breeze it goes further but still only a metre or so. If it is particularly gusty, however, the seeds can travel a fair bit further. Indeed, when a gusty blast of wind hits the small meadow you can see many parachutes or clusters of chutes, backlit by the sun, lifted 2 or 3m into the air and buffeted about. Some of these travel out of sight over the fence, hopefully to land safely and start a new colony.

Figure 6.13. *A Cat's-ear flower opening. Top left: Day one and the outermost ring of florets open. Top right: Day two and the second ring opens. Middle left: Day four and four rings are open. Middle right: Day seven and all the floret rings have opened. Bottom left: Three weeks or so later and the open clock has partly dispersed. Bottom right: A parachute from above showing how ragged and open it is.*

Figure 6.14. *A bedeguar gall on dog rose, a common plant in meadow hedges.*

By the time summer is well under way our dog roses (*Rosa canina*) (Figure 5.11) have finished their main flowering. As they usually flower in June and July, they have a season that spans both spring and summer. While the flowers may have finished, another rather intriguing decoration takes their place. This is variously called bedeguar gall, moss gall, or Robin's pin cushion. This latter name refers to Robin Goodfellow, who was a woodland sprite. A typical gall is shown in Figure 6.14.

This gall is created by a small wasp that is only 4mm long, *Diplolepis rosae*. The story is not as simple as a butterfly laying eggs on a plant that the caterpillar then eats as this wasp is parthenogenetic, with males being very rare. Parthenogenesis is a process whereby eggs can develop without being fertilised. The female lays her eggs, often around fifty, in the terminal leaf bud of a dog rose. When the eggs hatch the wasp larvae stimulate the distorted bud to overgrow in an apparently chaotic way. It is the cells associated with the excessive growth that the larvae feed on. The growth of the gall results in a ball that takes on the appearance of moss and is very distinctive.

The larvae overwinter in the gall, which will have shrivelled and died in the autumn. In May, the new wasps start to emerge from the old brown gall. We have considerable numbers of these wasps and their fluffy galls, especially in dry years as plants that have been stressed by drought seem particularly susceptible to attack. Because our soil is so light, the dog roses are regularly stressed by the availability of water gradually reducing as summer progresses.

In late summer, devil's-bit scabious (*Succisa pratensis*) has grown tall in the small meadow and is flowering. For most of the year the plant lives more or less at ground level as a rosette of narrow elliptical leaves of anything from five to 30cm in length. Although the flower shoot actually starts to extend in mid-April, growth then is very slow and it is not until July that it really accelerates. By mid to late August when the flowers begin to open the stalk is quite tall, up to a metre in height, with long, sparse, thin branches each finishing with a rounded, tightly packed head of dark blue-purple flowers. These flowers are magnets for insects, especially hoverflies, and devil's-bit is an important source of food for pollinators in the late summer when most other wildflowers are past their peak flowering period (Figure 6.15). It is also the food plant for the larvae of two rather striking and rather rare insects, marsh fritillary butterfly (*Euphydryas aurinia*) and narrow-bordered bee hawkmoth (*Hemaris tityus*), although, unfortunately, neither of these are found in our meadows.

Although still quite common, devil's-bit has probably declined quite significantly in this country, as it has elsewhere where traditional meadows have been lost. In the Netherlands changes in land use are thought to be responsible for its 75% decline in the last eighty years. Since the rosette of leaves is down at ground level and still needs access to light to produce food for the plant, devil's-bit struggles if the surrounding vegetation is not cut or grazed down each year. On the other hand, it is well adapted to the meadow environment, with the rosette being fairly resistant to trampling and its flattened leaves being protected from grazing. Trampling and cutting also prepares the ground for seedling establishment, which is the primary method devil's-bit uses for dispersal. It only occasionally spreads vegetatively by producing short rhizomes up to about 10cm in length. When its habitat deteriorates, because grazing or cutting for hay is reduced or stopped, or artificial fertiliser is added, growth is inhibited, seed set is reduced and seedling establishment is impeded. Even cutting the hay late, in August, can badly affect devil's-bit because its main source of propagation, seed, is cut off. A study in Swedish meadows found that the population growth rate of devil's-bit was 1.03 in grazed sites and 0.9 in non-grazed sites. In other words, where there was grazing the population was very gradually growing and where there was no grazing it was gradually shrinking. It may take a long time, but many places that appear to have a healthy population of devil's-bit today may eventually lose them if the habitat is sub-optimal. For example, if grazing is stopped in a pasture with 10,000 plants, at a growth rate of 0.9, devil's-bit would not die out for eighty-seven years. In practical

Figure 6.15. *Most gardeners will know that scabious plants are magnets for insects, and our wild devil's-bit scabious is no exception. Bees, like the common carder bumblebee (***Bombus pascuorum***) (top left), enjoy its late summer flowers, but hoverflies especially find it irresistible:* **Volucella inanis** *(middle left),* **Volucella pellucens** *(bottom left),* **Eristalis tenax**, *common drone fly (top right),* **Eristalis** *sp (second right),* **Epistrophe grossulariae** *(third right),* **Syrphus** *sp (bottom right).*

terms, with the abandonment of meadows mostly occurring around the middle of the last century, we may have many of these remnant populations on the verge of extinction. One of the aspects of our hay cut is that by doing it by hand we can steer around those plants still in flower. The two species that most often remain in flower as we enjoy the late summer cut are knapweeds and the few scabious plants that we have. By exercising care with our cutter, we hope to stop the decline in scabious numbers and maintain these lovely flowers.

Producing seed, then, is key for devil's-bit scabious and, although it is self-fertile, out-crossing is best at promoting seed set. This means pollinators are crucial and for devil's-bit hoverflies seem to be the prime movers in the role; one study found devil's-bit pollen made up more than 50% of the total load attached to their bodies. How does the hoverfly find the scabious? The majority of flies are attracted to flowers by a mixture of sight and smell, with visual attraction operating at the longest range and flower colour being the primary visual cue. Flies see a different colour spectrum to humans, and with a different emphasis. They can see UV, which we cannot, and then all through the spectrum up to yellow, but they cannot see red, and their colour vision is focused into four channels: broadly UV, blue, purple and green. One of the most common drone flies to visit devil's-bit is, perhaps unsurprisingly, common drone fly (*Eristalis tenax*). Its colour preferences are first yellow, then blue, green and UV. Although it has an innate preference for yellow, flies, like bees, are known to learn which flowers are good food sources and once it has discovered rewarding blue flowers the common drone fly's yellow preference disappears. The devil's-bit flower colour does seem to be enhanced for attracting these flies by having a greater contrast between the colour channels to which flies are sensitive. The overall flower shape may also help flies to find them. The heavy flower heads on the end of long thin stalks will sway easily and a fly's vision, which is not so good at resolving shape, is remarkable at perceiving motion.

The change of season from summer to cooler autumn is imperceptible, until the early mornings become cold and the days shorten and we realise that summer is over. This change of season does not mean that the meadow stops, but it does slow down. Eventually we cannot pretend any longer that summer is hanging on; the plants have stopped growing and leaves are starting to show a tinge of autumn colour. Those annuals that remained uncut during haymaking are starting to droop, with rain helping the process, and the butterflies are gone for this year.

CHAPTER 7

Meadows in autumn and winter

During the autumn the meadow slows down and during the winter it is at its quietest. This is not to say that it is silent, or that there is nothing going on, but it is a restful time of year for the meadow. As far as we are concerned, autumn is the time to put the meadow to bed, to make it ready for the spring when the meadow will be busy with new activity and we should try not to disturb it any more than is absolutely necessary.

Probably the biggest event in the large meadow in the autumn, in fact the biggest event of the year, is the annual cut. Sometimes there will be another cut during the spring, but it is best if a cut is made in the autumn and then the meadow left to rest and recuperate through the winter. By autumn, the long summer days will have noticeably shortened and the temperatures, especially at night, dropped. This shortening of daylight hours with lower temperatures triggers the onset of plant senescence as well as reducing the ability of insects to fly. Some species, such as some bumblebees, will fly right through the autumn period until there is no point in foraging further, at which point they will hibernate. While they are generally social animals, living in colonies, they overwinter as lone queen bees. The new queen will go into hibernation as soon as she has reached a heavy enough body weight. To survive her six- to eight-month hibernation she needs to be 0.6 to 0.8g, losing 50% of her weight while hibernating. Queens weighing less than 0.6g at the start of hibernation will not usually survive. Those that do will come out of hibernation in spring and almost immediately start searching for a nest site. Most species nest somewhere underground, perhaps an old wood mouse (*Apodemus sylvaticus*) burrow or a cavity at the base of a wall. Once settled in she makes and fills a wax honey pot, and a pollen and honey ball to lay her first batch of eggs on. The honey pot feeds her when periods of inclement weather prevent foraging and while brooding the egg ball. Once hatched the larvae feed almost exclusively on pollen, while adults feed almost exclusively on nectar.

With the change of seasons food supplies will change as well, so our badgers (*Meles meles*) will be eating more blackberries as they become available, as, too, will many birds. Another, and possibly more surprising, consumer of low-lying blackberries are foxes (*Vulpes vulpes*). By far the biggest consumer of the ripening fruit are the late insects, who lap up the sweet and sticky juices. Butterflies and beetles, flies and wasps all share in the bounty.

Bramble (*Rubus fruticosus* agg.) plants form an important part of the hedge line in the large meadow and we wait for the blackberries to finish before cutting them back. This is a species for which the epithet 'invasive' could have been coined. Brambles don't just spread by seeds, but also by leapfrogging. The tendrils can extend long distances in graceful arcs and when they touch down, if they are undisturbed and the ground is damp, they root. This ostensibly creates another plant, the linking growth becoming unnecessary for survival. By having both roots and attachment to the parent plant supplying water and nutrients, the clonal offshoot can grow with enormous vigour. Just like with bracken (*Pteridium aquilinum*) and nettles (*Urtica dioica*), attempted eradication is a fruitless activity, but keeping them under control will allow them to provide autumn food and cover for all manner of birds and animals. We discovered early on that control of brambles is complicated by the retained blackberry seeds on the plants when they are cut. This is also compounded by brambles being another of nature's own barbed wire.

Under normal circumstances, cut material that cannot be distributed as seed stock to other meadows or sold as fodder can be stacked and left to compact down. In the past this would be described as being left to rot, but this is not so. The process does start as rotting, but eventually slows right down almost to a stop, after which the carbon is effectively sequestered for a very long period, just as it is in peat bogs. This is exactly what we wanted to do with the cut brambles. Unfortunately, these were not just a few prunings that would have been easy to deal with, this was a large cut-back to stop and partially reverse the invasion of the body of the meadow. This amount of bramble was almost impossible to handle; also the introduction of seeds into our pile of cut grass on such a scale would make dealing with it the following year even more difficult. So we reluctantly decided that it would have to be burnt. We did this as close to the cutting area as possible, which allowed us to control the burn and create a considerable amount of charcoal, rather than just smoke and carbon dioxide. The benefit of this is similar to making biochar; it does not return all the carbon to the atmosphere as carbon dioxide and the charcoal can be dug into the ground, where it will hold the carbon for many years.

The method and equipment you choose for cutting your meadow will depend on many factors, from the area you have to the time you can give to it. If you are short of time and have a large area, a contractor with a tractor is one solution, but for smaller areas you may want to take a more leisurely approach. This can be by using smaller powered equipment, or even a hand scythe (Figure 7.1). A scythe has many advantages, the primary two being giving exercise and the ability to cut right up to fence posts and tree trunks.

Figure 7.1. *Small self-propelled scissor cutters (left) can be used on quite large plots and a scythe (right) for small plots and tricky areas not readily accessible with machinery.*

You should not mistake the meadow hay cut for a modern silage cut as they are quite different. Modern silage cuts, taken several times a year, are a method of generating feedstock on an industrial scale, but from fields of very low diversity. They can hardly be described as meadows and they are always monotonous (Figure 7.2).

When you cut your meadow you are actively distributing the plant seeds and removing the vegetation that would otherwise remain and slowly limit the amount of diversity you have. The cut material that you collect has a considerable residual seed content and if you know anyone who wants to start a meadow it can be offered to them for spreading on their own land. The method used does not need to be sophisticated; the cuttings can simply be spread on the land and the seeds left to fall to the ground in their own time.

The collecting method that you use will also depend upon the size of the meadow and how much time you are prepared to put into clearing your cut hay. It is worth considering how robust your ground is. Our soil is very light, so we move the dry hay using a simple boat of a sheet tied at both ends (Figure 7.3). This spreads the load across a wide surface and can be dragged across cut or uncut ground without leaving anything more than the lightest of tracks. This is in stark contrast to wheeled vehicles

Figure 7.2. *Modern silage production.*

carrying the same load that can slip and dislodge the surface vegetation, and will flatten and break any foliage they run across.

Like many meadows, ours produces ostensibly delightful hay, but it cannot be used as food for livestock as it contains ragwort (*Jacobaea vulgaris*), although this makes no difference to the value of the hay for recreating a meadow elsewhere. You may think that the hay is simply a transit method for the introduction of seeds to other fields, but it is more intricate than that. Because your meadow will have been left without toxins or fertilisers, when the foliage is cut, it will contain all sorts of small creatures. These will be predominantly insects, but also spiders and other arthropods. The range of small creatures will be in the form of nymphs, such as grasshoppers and shield bugs, eggs, from all sorts of insects, and caterpillars or pupae from moths and butterflies (Figure 7.4). Some species are not so easily moved and can only be expected to make the move to a new site as adults, under their own power. One such is the very easily spotted butterfly, the marbled white (*Melanargia galathea*). This delightful flying chequerboard has a caterpillar that feeds on our meadow grasses, but pupates at ground level, lodged safely against the weather in among the root ball of the grass that it fed on through the summer.

Even while we are raking the hay in the warm autumn days, the ageing grasshoppers are becoming sluggish. They have been laying their eggs in the soil to stay safe until

Figure 7.3. *A 'boat' made from a tied sheet that can be used for moving hay over delicate foliage and terrain.*

they emerge as nymphs in the spring. This is another way in which species will avoid being translocated with cut hay. Of course, if you cut your meadow when there are still adults about, some will be moved and some of these may be ready to lay eggs. In which case the following year the new meadow will almost miraculously ring to the sound of grasshoppers in its very first year. During the autumn the noise of summer insects declines slowly, wasps get slower and bumblebees fewer.

From the summer onwards our buzzards (*Buteo buteo*) start flying as a family group. Usually there are four in the wake, two adults and two young birds, but sometimes when times are harder, there are only three as a lack of food takes its toll on the young birds. Our buzzards stay all year round, although this is not the case with all of them as some migrate to lands further south. The mewling calls of the buzzards make a pleasing soundtrack to the quiet and contemplative process of raking the autumn cut. While raking the cut grass, which will have dried out over a few days, I have disturbed slow worms (*Anguis fragilis*), which quite surprised me as I had never considered the possibility of having reptiles in the meadow. I have also disturbed field voles (*Microtus agrestis*). Although one of our most common mammals, it is really quite secretive and, due to a quirk of anatomy, until they rush off it is not always easy to tell which end is which. With a population of about 75 million, the field vole outnumbers humans as well as most other mammal species.

Figure 7.4. *A moth pupa attached to grass in a meadow. This will be carried with the cut stalk to the next field, where it can be strewn to start another meadow. Although seeds are most often considered as the major component of strewn meadow foliage, insects and spiders will also be present.*

During the autumn, fungal fruiting bodies become more apparent. Some are low to the ground and are only seen when the grass is cut short. Common earthball, *Scleroderma citrinum*, is just such a fungus (Figure 7.5).

This particular fungus is responsible for a large proportion of the poisonings associated with eating wild fungi. As it is closely related to the giant puffball (*Calvatia gigantea*), both genetically and in appearance, and has a similar period of growth, from July to November, the common earthball is regularly mistaken for the delicious giant puffball. Earthballs have an associated parasitic fungus, the parasitic bolete (*Pseudoboletus parasiticus*), which, although we do not find it in our meadow, is worth looking out for as this rare toadstool is dependent on the earthballs for survival and although it is edible, it is not very palatable.

Figure 7.5. *A common earthball in our meadow with fully exposed spores.*

By 1 October autumn has definitely set in, you can feel it in the air and the parrot waxcaps (*Gliophorus psittacinus*) are trouping in the small meadow. Parrot waxcap is small, slimy and brightly coloured. It can be a rich green or yellow or a mixture of the two but almost always with some green. Other waxcaps grow in the small meadow as well, some producing toadstools as early as the end of July. By my estimate, the small meadow has a sufficient variety of fungi to be placed in Plantlife's 'may be of grassland interest' category (Figure 7.6). Fungal fruit bodies are the classic reminder of the unseen activity going on under our feet in 'that dark laboratory', as the ecologist Aldo Leopold described the soil. Fungi dominate life underground in the same way that plants dominate it above ground, these two groups working closely together. As much as 30% of the space close to roots is occupied by fungi and close to 90% of plant species are believed to form a symbiotic relationship, called mycorrhiza (fungus root), with fungi. The fungus forms a sheath around the plant's roots and grows its hyphae inside the root to varying extents depending on the type of mycorrhiza. Outside the sheath the fungus's hyphae explore the soil. Think of hyphae as the fungus's cells, very long and very thin, like tiny filaments. They are much finer than the thinnest root hairs and so they can grow into nooks and crannies that plant roots cannot reach. They also have a much bigger surface area than roots, and excrete enzymes that break down components of the soil around them. This makes the fungus far superior to the plant at absorbing water and nutrients from the soil, so the plant then takes these from the fungus. On the other hand, fungi cannot photosynthesize and so the plant provides them with sugars, much of which is converted to a glycoprotein called glomalin that is thought to be important for carbon storage.

All this is relatively well understood in general, but the relationship between individual fungi and plant species is still rather mysterious, especially when it comes to waxcaps. Originally waxcaps were assumed to be saprotrophs, members of the huge guild of fungi that get their sugar by breaking down dead vegetation, the various wood rots, for instance, but there is now good evidence that this is not the case. Then it was suggested that they are mycorrhizal on mosses and while this seems to be true for some, it definitely does not apply to all. Recent evidence suggests that they are in a kind of evolutionary mid-state between the saprotrophs and the mycorrhizae, but closer to the latter because they do get a certain amount of sugar from living plants.

There is an interesting, though unanswered, question regarding why waxcap fruiting bodies should be characteristically brightly coloured and slimy? Just as for their detailed lifestyles, the reasons behind form and function in specific fungi is still largely a mystery, and also a particular trait may have several functions. Colour pigments, for example, are expensive for the fungus to make, so they must be important, and they are multifunctional, potentially being warning signals, anti-bacterial, anti-oxidant and so on. In waxcaps, the slime is thought to be partly protection against desiccation and partly to discourage browsers, and one function

Figure 7.6. *Fungi of the small meadow. Top left: Parrot waxcap* (**Gliophorus psittacinus**)*. Top right: Slimy waxcap* (**Gliophorus irrigatus**)*. Middle left: Spangle waxcap* (**Hygrocybe insipida**) *Middle right: Snowy waxcap* (**Cuphophyllus virgineus**) *Bottom left: Apricot club* (**Clavulinopsis luteoalba**) *Bottom right: Common conecap* (**Conocybe tenera**)*.*

of the bright colours is as a warning because they produce toxins. Consequently, most of them are rated as either inedible or poisonous.

In areas with short grass, like the small meadow after the hay cut, the autumn coaxes out a different-looking type of fungus, the fairy club fungi (Figure 7.6 bottom left). These are very difficult to see if the herbage is more than a few centimetres tall as they are easily hidden. They grow on unimproved acidic grassland, sometimes in quite large amounts, hidden by the grasses. They are also generally regarded as mycorrhizal species, many of them associated with trees.

While many living things slow down as night-time temperatures drop and the days start to shorten noticeably, wasps become rather less discerning about who they sting when they are disturbed. They give a good impression of an irascible animal with pent up energy and aggression, so it is best to give their nests a wide berth. Besides, they will quite likely reuse the site next year as queens will hibernate in the old nest. Some will move on and can be recognised by their size as they fly across the meadow looking for hibernating sites. Although they are bigger than the workers, which are also females, they cannot be confused with hornets, which are much bigger, brown and yellow, rather than black and yellow, and rather more easy-going than wasps. However, I do have it on good authority that if you are stung by a hornet it is much, much worse than a wasp sting. The naturalist that was on the receiving end of this did say that while it is much more painful, it would not be recommended to use this as a basis for a taxonomic identification.

It is 8 October, sunny and, at 20°C, hot for October. There are banded snails glued to old plant stems about 15cm off the ground (Figure 7.7). Could they be hibernating? These snails are the stripy multicoloured sort, usually with black bands. Both of the common garden species of banded snail live in the small meadow. These particular ones have a black band across the lip of the shell opening, which makes them dark-lipped banded snails (*Cepaea nemoralis*). There are times when snails seal the opening of their shell with a thick layer of mucus that, when it dries, acts both as a glue to hold them in place and a waterproof covering, as much to keep water in as to keep it out. When they do this in summer it is because it is too hot and dry and they are protecting themselves from becoming desiccated. When they do it in the autumn it is to move into hibernation before the cold of winter strikes. On both occasions they retreat back into their shells and sit out the bad weather.

These two periods of shelter, aestivation in the summer and hibernation in the winter, are vital for survival of snails because desiccation will kill them quite quickly. Snails and slugs are the only land-living members of the molluscs, which are primarily aquatic animals. The slime they cover themselves with is hygroscopic, it attracts water rather than repelling it, but it cannot cope with dry conditions. Snails also suffer severely from predation, juveniles from shrews, toads and frogs, adults from birds, especially thrushes, and small mammals, and eggs from almost anything that can

Figure 7.7. *A Dark-lipped banded snail on a yellow rattle* (**Rhinanthus minor**) *seed head. The snail is either going into hibernation or has died during aestivation.*

get access to them. These survival issues mean that snails are quite prolific breeders. Adult dark-lipped banded snails lay between two and three broods per year, with roughly forty eggs per brood. Because they are hermaphrodite, every snail being both male and female, after mating each of the pair is able to lay eggs. Against this must be balanced the low survival rate of the eggs. Only about 50% of summer broods and 10% of winter broods survive, whole batches can be wiped out if a predator happens upon them and winter frosts can kill them. Among juveniles there is at least a further 55% mortality. It takes one to two years for a snail to become a sexually mature adult, and, although a dark-lipped banded snail can live for up to six years in the wild, the average age at death is just two. Overall, in a diverse and stable system, the population of living snails will reach a constant level and thus continually play a part in recycling dead or dying plant material, as well as providing this abundance of food for other members of the community.

Dead snails are very useful to the community, too. Birds need a rich source of calcium to make their egg shells and their normal diet is calcium poor. Obviously the shell is the last part of the egg to be made and so just before laying birds will search out one of the richest sources of calcium available to them, empty snail shells. Great tits have been seen shell hunting and in Holland, when acid rain was responsible for reducing the number of snails, great tits struggled to produce eggs with normal shells. Empty snail shells are also used as nest sites by some solitary bees, like the two-coloured mason bee (*Osmia bicolor*). If the shell is big enough, the bee will lay up to five eggs in it, each in an individual cell made from plant material and provisioned with honey. The bee covers the entrance with the same material, and the whole shell with a disguise: a thatch of twigs and other bits of vegetation woven together with moss.

When the sward is short in winter, the presence of worms in the meadow's soil becomes obvious from the casts they throw up (Figure 7.8). Charles Darwin was fascinated by earthworms and he spent forty years or so studying them on his land around Down House. His work culminated in a best-selling book on the subject that concluded 'it may be doubted whether there are many other animals which have played so important a part in the history of the world, as have these lowly organised creatures'. He was enthralled by the earthworm's ability to bury objects merely by tunnelling beneath them in the normal course of their lives. For example, in one old pasture near Down House he found that fragments of chalk rock became buried to a depth of 18cm over twenty-nine years, that is 6mm per year. The common earthworm (*Lumbricus terrestris*) is most frequently responsible for the worm casts we see in this country and was probably the type making most of the casts around Down House.

While snails operate at ground level, earthworms operate below ground level, where they are some of the largest subterranean invertebrates. Earthworms accelerate the decomposition of leaf litter and other plant material, enhancing nutrient recycling

Figure 7.8. *A common earthworm disappearing into its tunnel beneath its cast in the small meadow.*

and water movement through the soil. This improves soil structure, increasing beneficial microbial activity. Much of this is achieved simply by the way they feed. They tunnel through the soil taking in plant material, mineral particles and microbes, mix these with mucus and enzymes, and grind this altogether using the mineral particles in a very strong gizzard. What comes out at the far end is a rich, friable, aggregate of organic and mineral frass, which is what we see as a worm cast.

A symbiotic link between worms and bacteria adds a very significant secondary contribution to the ecosystem engineering. This has been called the Sleeping Beauty Paradox because dormant microbes are woken up by the earthworm when they are taken into its gut. The digestion of the plant material is then facilitated by the microbes. All this activity enhances plant growth by providing access to nutrients. These microbe symbionts also produce chemicals that affect plant development, such as flowering and fruiting, by triggering hormone production.

The common earthworm makes casts by tunnelling vertically and dragging leaves and other vegetation down into the tunnel for pre-digestion and eventual incorporation into the soil. Other species work horizontally either in the surface litter or underground, and they too produce a similar frass but this is not built into casts. Species burrowing horizontally in the surface litter are especially good at recycling phosphorus, while the horizontal-burrowing sub-surface species are good at recycling nitrogen. Not surprisingly, the best soils for plant growth are produced when worms of all three different types are present. Darwin estimated that more than 9 tonnes dry weight of soil passes through the earthworms in every acre every year, enough so that the whole surface layer passes through them every few years. Using Darwin's estimate of the number of earthworms in every acre, the global total weighs approximately ten times all humanity, and with more recent data this is believed to be a gross underestimate.

When earthworms come to the surface, usually at night and when it is wet, they provide a food supply for nocturnal species. Badgers love them. Those that find themselves stranded during the day are often taken by birds, some of them perhaps by the jays (*Garrulus glandarius*) that visit the small meadow in autumn and winter (Figure 7.9). More likely the jays have come to bury acorns or to eat the acorns they have buried. Jays and wood mice are the two specialist hoarders of acorns and are most likely to be responsible for planting the oak seedlings that spring up well away from oak trees. Even though they bury acorns in the open, jays are really woodland birds and in less wooded places where they are not so common, other corvids, such as magpies (*Pica pica*) and rooks (*Corvus frugilegus*), which are known to bury acorns occasionally, may be responsible. We believe it is magpies that plant the acorns in the large meadow, because jays are rarely seen here.

Figure 7.9. *A Jay prospecting the small meadow.*

The jay is actually an opportunist omnivore, eating whatever is seasonal: seeds, fruits and berries, insects, birds' eggs, young birds, bats and small rodents. Cached acorns are a very important component of its winter diet, with fewer jays surviving the winter in years when the mast is poor. If it is offered acorns in spring and summer a jay will eat most and just store a few for a short time, while in the autumn it will store most of them without eating them. With its good, long memory, aided by often burying the acorns near a visual landmark or by placing a visual cue, like a stick, close by, the jay is able to retrieve from its caches year round. Some acorns are forgotten though, or they germinate before being retrieved, which is not surprising when you consider that one bird can bury between 2,000 and 6,000 every autumn, one per cache across their whole territory, which can be up to 100 hectares. Cache sites are usually between 3 and 500 metres from the tree, although if the jay is feeding outside its territory it can bring acorns back from several kilometres away.

By the end of the winter there will be very few acorns left on the ground beneath an oak tree and vanishingly few of those will germinate when left lying on the soil surface. This means that the whole crop has either been eaten or hoarded, hence hoarding must be essential for oak regeneration. Experiments have shown that the two big seed leaves that fill most of the acorn are bigger than needed to sustain the germination process. In fact, they have probably evolved especially to attract animals to help with dispersal while at the same time distracting them from the rest of the embryo. Acorns that have had part of their cotyledons eaten and even seedlings that have had them completely eaten off, continue to survive and grow perfectly well. A jay is quite an expert oak horticulturist. It carefully selects an open and exposed habitat like short grassland to bury acorns individually. It buries only the healthiest acorns, pushing them about 1.5 cm into the soil, which happens to be the ideal depth for germination.

Despite all of these growing aids provided by jays, most of the cached acorns or young seedlings will die in one way or another. This is hardly surprising since every hectare of oak woodland can produce over 600kg of acorns a year. Nonetheless, in these days of mass tree planting it is worth considering just what a valuable service the jay is providing. In Sweden it has been calculated the cost of humans planting the same number of oaks as one pair of jays would be between £4,500 and £17,000, depending on the methods used. What is more, the jays do this continuously over wide areas, something that would be difficult and more costly still for humans.

As the winter progresses, the weather will be colder and wetter, which makes the ground delicate and very easy to churn into mud. So at this time of year, if you have any light soil, or soil that is easily waterlogged, staying off it is a good idea, especially with machinery. This is not always possible, especially if you are planting hedges. Hedging is very definitely an autumn and winter activity, when the plants have lost their leaves and are more or less dormant (Figure 7.10). The thing about hedging is

Figure 7.10. *A very early-stage hedge. This will take several years before it is ready for layering into a fully formed livestock-proof hedge.*

that it has to be approached in the same way as planting trees. While it can be done at other times of the year, if it is carried out in the autumn or winter it is not generally necessary to water the plants as by the time the dry weather starts in the spring, they should have set down growing roots and be self-sufficient. This is not always the case with the soil in the large meadow as it is very light and inclined to dry out in the early part of the year if there are a few days without rain. This can reduce the survival rate of your nascent hedge by a considerable amount. If you do not have a large length of boundary to hedge, there is a method that can be used that guarantees a better result, but is very labour intensive. This is to retain your hedging plants in either water, or in pots, until there is root growth. At this point they can be planted in the hedge line and as long as it is no later than March it should give quite a good outcome. Many hedging techniques require individual plants of the newly created hedge to be wrapped around as protection against being eaten by rabbits (*Oryctolagus cuniculus*) and seasonal grazers, either your own or wild species like deer. There is another way, however, if you have a considerable growth of grass and taller plants in the hedge line. Just plant the hedging and let it get on with it. One of the constantly sold ideas in the twentieth and twenty-first centuries is of the instant product, and this even extends to hedges. Instead, you could do what the jays and magpies do for oak and seed your hedge line with hawthorn and sloe and all the other species that you would expect to find. It will take longer to develop, but will be all the more interesting during the process than simply planting hedging.

While autumn and winter are good times for planting and planning, taking stock of the meadow is time well spent. Creating a meadow or a hedgerow takes time. The plants, animals and land have their own idea of who should grow where, and to believe that a hedge has been created by massive planting or a meadow by stripping top soil and reseeding is a mistake. Creating either is a much more gentle process and is best carried out on a timescale of years so that the balance of plants and animals within the field is not upset. Actions carried out in the dormant months can have long-term repercussions that will not be noticed until the meadow wakes up in the spring.

Part Four

CHAPTER 8

Ecology and species interactions in a meadow

One of the most interesting thing about our meadows is that it has brought home to us something that we already knew, but did not fully understand. Ecology is not just about the interaction between two different species, in fact it is not even about the interaction between several species, it is about the whole picture. It was only during the second half of the twentieth century that any clear idea of ecology as we now understand it was formed. This was despite the word first being used in 1866 by Ernst Haeckel in Germany. When first considered, ecology was as simple as describing where a species lived, or what it fed upon. Indeed, until recently it was popularly thought that ecology was just the interaction of one species with another, but now we know better. The way species interact and react to each other can be complicated and unexpected, and sometimes they will have an effect on each other without any direct contact between them.

An example of a simple association between meadow species is shown by a rather striking hoverfly (*Scaeva pyrastri*) (Figure 8.1). This has a larva that looks something like a caterpillar and feeds on the aphids that live on meadow plants such as knapweeds and ragworts. Aphids can significantly weaken the plants and reduce their nectar production; these are the same plants that provide food for the adult fly.

This simple relationship between aphids and hoverflies is often seen as pivotal for gardeners controlling aphids, but there is obviously more to it than that. If it was that simple, then there would only be one species of hoverfly eating aphids.

When looking at an ecological system it is worth having an idea of what ecology is in a scientific context. Broadly speaking, it is about the interactions between species and between populations, but it does not depend upon knowing all of the species present in an area. It can, for example, be considered in terms of the nutrient cycle. This can be framed in terms of the types of organisms present, rather than species, but the broader these groupings are, the more imprecise and oversimplified the results will be. For example, it is possible to put all the soil fungi together, even though they have a huge range of activities, from actively catching nematode worms in the soil,

Figure 8.1. *The hoverfly* **Scaeva pyrastri**, *whose larvae help to keep aphids in check on the food plants of the adult.*

through the toadstool-producing species that we come across on damp mornings, to symbiotic species that are essential for seed germination of orchids. Another method used to look at an ecology is to consider the energy flows within the whole community of plant and animal species. As can be appreciated, this is rather difficult and cannot tell you anything about all the interactions that do not involve energy movement.

What we can say with some certainty is that just knowing about individual species is not enough to understand an ecology. This is not to imply that natural history in its basic form of finding and listing all the species in a specific environment is not a valid and enjoyable activity. Doing this will give a fairly clear idea of the complexity of an ecosystem, although not the interactions between all the organisms that are there.

A species list can be of particular value when you want to watch the changing nature of your meadow, or, on a longer and wider scale, the changes associated with climate. Studying an individual species closely can also contribute to the development of an overall picture of the activity that goes on within a meadow. A good example of this increasing the understanding of meadows and what goes on in them can be found in the example of the large blue butterfly (*Phengaris arion*).

By 1979 the large blue was said to be extinct in Great Britain. This is the largest blue butterfly that is to be found in the UK. You notice that the tense suggests it can still be found, that is because it was quietly, and successfully, reintroduced in the

Figure 8.2. *Large blue (left) and pearl-bordered fritillary (right) butterflies. These illustrations are taken from* British Butterflies *by W.S. Coleman, published in 1867.*

1980s. Where large blues and pearl-bordered fritillaries (*Boloria euphrosyne*) coexist, an interesting and unexpected interaction can be found (Figure 8.2).

The large blue suffered badly from collecting, in fact in the nineteenth century it was already recognised that it was extremely local. Even while it was being collected to extinction, little was known of its life cycle, even the food and appearance of the caterpillar was unknown. The complexity of the large blue life cycle was part of the reason that the nineteenth-century naturalists were in the dark about the caterpillar. For it to thrive it is necessary for there to be two other species present; an ant called *Myrmica sabuleti* and wild thyme (*Thymus drucei*).

Large blue butterflies lay their eggs on thyme, and *Myrmica* ants take thyme seeds into their nests as food. What happens next is quite extraordinary. The caterpillars hatch and feed on the thyme until the larva reaches the fourth instar. At this point the caterpillar drops to the ground, where it is found by the ants. These then pick up the larva and take it into the nest, where it changes diet and continues to grow by feeding on ant larvae. When the caterpillar is fully grown, it pupates, eventually leaving the nest as an adult butterfly. One of the unexpected consequences of this convoluted life cycle is that *Myrmica sabuleti* will desert a nest if it is overly infected with a large number of caterpillars, probably because of the large loss of ant larvae. When the ants leave, the remaining thyme seeds germinate and, in following years, when they flower they increase the food stock for the adult pearl-bordered fritillaries. This butterfly then lay its eggs on dog violets. So increasing numbers of large blue butterflies can increase the amount of thyme plants and indirectly increase the numbers of pearl-bordered fritillaries.

When initial attempts were made to preserve the dwindling number of large blue populations, mistakes were made associated directly with a lack of understanding about the various species involved. Wild thyme and its ant *Myrmica sabuleti* are both species that thrive in short grass. When the conservationists decided, with the best of intentions, to protect the last colonies of large blue butterflies by fencing off the area, grazers were excluded, the grass grew too tall, the ants disappeared and with them went the butterflies.

It is the diversity of meadows that seems to add a level of protection for each species and helps avoid catastrophic variations in population numbers. It may seem counter-intuitive, but in ecological terms, the way in which you manage your meadow will increase its biodiversity and, consequently, its stability, not just by increasing the species numbers, but also by de-synchronising the biological links between species. When looking at a meadow you will often notice staggered flowering. This may be only small pockets of plants, but something in the soil, or the way it is maintained, has resulted in not all the plants synchronising their flowering period. The alternative situation is frequently found in commercial agriculture, where synchronising growth and seed production in monoculture crops is necessary for efficient use of mechanised harvesting. These are less stable as anything that affects a single plant can be expected to affect all the plants. So by de-synchronising the plants and animals in a meadow you are, in effect, increasing the stability in the same way as increasing the number of species will. We have a practical example of this that took place in our large meadow by accident.

The grass in our large meadow, of about 1.5 hectares, was slowly being controlled by gradually increasing amounts of yellow rattle (*Rhinanthus minor*) and timed cuts. Although we had introduced the yellow rattle, it had been left to seed and spread at its own pace. Unfortunately, in the middle of flowering in 2019 horses from the next field, seeing that our grass was greener, managed to force the fence down. They had been feeding for a couple of days before the alarm was raised and I was able to get them removed. During the time they were in residence they managed to eat a large amount of the yellow rattle that was in flower at the bottom of the field, an area both sunny and sheltered. However, at the top of the meadow was an area that had not yet come into flower and these plants were ignored. The disparity in flowering time, although of only a few days, saved us from a total loss of our yellow rattle. We did have to re-seed the bottom area, using seed from the top of the meadow, as well as making sure the fences were not so easily damaged by a horse leaning against the posts. It took two years to regain the same level of control over the grass because as soon as the horses were removed the grass started to grow, unchecked by grazing or rattle, but additionally fertilised by the horses.

One of the first demonstrations of synchronicity was between two different species in the same area, rather than a lack of synchronicity within a single species in a single area as shown by my yellow rattle. This experiment was described in 1924 by C.S. Elton. He was looking at the relationship between population numbers of snowshoe hares (*Lepus americanus*) and its natural predator, the Canada lynx (*Lynx canadensis*). The names of these two protagonists are interesting. The Canada lynx comes from Canada, as you would expect. The snowshoe hare, on the other hand, takes its name from its very large hind feet, that act like snowshoes to stop the hare from sinking in the snow. What Elton demonstrated is something that we probably take for granted now, that the population densities of lynx and hare are intimately linked, each one influencing the other. When the hare population went up, the lynx population would also go up, but lagging a little behind. Although a clear demonstration, it is a simple relationship observed in a relatively simple ecosystem. Such simple two species associations should not be significant in a complex system like a meadow. But, as happened to our meadow, introducing an unrestricted predator on an unsuspecting prey, like a horse with a weakness for yellow rattle, can have the same result with a local population collapse.

With a biodiverse system containing a large number of species, wide variations tend not to take place very rapidly. There are conditions, of course, where the population might crash, but this is often associated with a particularly severe weather event, perhaps a very cold or wet winter. Part of the value of a species-rich meadow lies in its diversity; it will naturally act as a buffer for all manner of fluctuations in predator, prey and weather. This is in stark contrast to the agricultural systems that rely on large-scale monoculture, as is the case with most arable crops, improved meadows and also modern orchards. It is not simply that there is only one crop involved, but also that the whole crop comes into flower and seeds at almost exactly the same time, it is synchronised. This is good for the farmer but only for as long as neither disease nor pest arrives. Because a large acreage of a single species will stimulate the rapid increase in disease or pest insect numbers, it therefore becomes necessary for the farmer to start a totally artificial campaign of chemical control.

In our own meadow the most noticeable fluctuations that we see are associated with butterflies. This is hardly surprising as these insects tend to be quite large and even small ones like skippers and blues are easily spotted. Consequently, it is possible to gain a relatively good idea of what sort of numbers are present on an annual basis. For us the easiest species to look at is the marbled white (*Melanargia galathea*), as it is a very distinctive insect (Figure 8.3) and its population numbers can be counted quite accurately. This is a species that arrived quite soon after we started actively managing the large meadow. It can fly well over relatively long distances looking for new breeding and feeding sites, which is how it came to us. This behaviour explains why butterflies are often seen apparently in transit crossing fields and gardens with a determined straight line of flight.

Marbled white butterflies have larvae that feed on grasses, hence the association with meadows. The preferred species are red fescue (*Festuca rubra*), sheep's fescue (*Festuca ovina*) and Yorkshire fog (*Holcus lanatus*). Of these we have red fescue and Yorkshire fog in abundance. They are quite tall grasses and although already present when we took over our meadow, they were marginalised as the presence of horses keeping the sward short and trampling the edges reduced the amount of these tall grasses that achieved their full size. Along with a proper system to both control the grass and allow it to flower and seed, we encouraged other insect food plants, like vetches, which provide both nectar for adults and food plants for larva. Another species that increased in numbers was the meadow brown (*Maniola jurtina*) (Figure 8.4). This is much more of a generalist species of grassland and, as one of our most common species, is widespread across the country. In fact, meadow brown turned up in the small meadow, too, once the lawn grass was allowed to grow up.

Although butterflies act as a very good 'canary in the mine' for the health of grassland, they do have a drawback in that there is a tendency to imagine these insects as just being associated with their food plants. This would effectively be the snowshoe hare and lynx situation. But meadows, once developed, are far more intricate than this in their ecological structure. Butterflies are easy to count, but as an organism the ecologically most significant part of their life cycle is the caterpillar. This has often been ignored because, as we have seen with the large blue butterfly, the caterpillar can remain relatively unknown, while the adults are simultaneously recorded, revered and collected sometimes to extinction. Besides the consumption of plant material that the caterpillar gets through, many of the caterpillars themselves

Figure 8.3. *Marbled white butterfly. It is in fact a 'brown' rather than a 'white' butterfly.*

Figure 8.4. *Meadow brown butterfly, one of the most common grassland species.*

will be food for other insects, spiders and birds. Blue tits, for example, consume vast quantities of caterpillars during the breeding season as they feed their young.

Butterfly populations are thought to react quickly to changes in the environment, not by calculation of course, but simply by responding to lack of food or suitable habitats for pupation. This fast response is associated with the rapid life cycle of butterflies. There are many other rapid turn-over species, but none so obvious in the environment as butterflies, and none so quickly noticed by their absence. In isolated meadows fragmented populations of butterflies may not be sustainable in the long-term without contact or interaction with other populations. This seems like a very reasonable assumption, but it is not always possible to be sure of this. Some species seem to be made up of such small populations that would appear not to be viable. One thing that does seem to be well established is the susceptibility to disease of populations that have been established by a very small number of founders. That this is not an absolute rule of biology can be seen in the entirely self-pollinated bee orchid (*Ophrys apifera*) (Figure 8.5), which seems to thrive in Northern Europe without its natural pollinator.

It goes almost without saying that one of the best ways to extend the range of both flora and fauna is by restoring existing habitats. This is not always easy as recent

Figure 8.5. *The self-pollinated bee orchid.*

agricultural practices have caused fragmentation of habitats, which carries with it a central problem. Restoring a meadow will give a superficial appearance of success, but if there are no extant meadow species ready to move into your new project, it will remain as a field entirely dependent upon what seeds you put in. The good news here is that hedgerows constitute a reservoir of species that will include meadow species. Also, in more recent times, it has become quite easy to purchase suitable seed from commercial suppliers.

Agricultural changes will tend to have a far greater effect on plants and animals that have a low population density. For these a small and subtle change in circumstances may severely damage a population, which can result in complete loss of that particular plant or animal in an area. If the nearest founding population of a species is too far away to get to the restored meadow, then it may never arrive, or only after a very long time. During this lapse, the fragility of the meadow ecosystem will be compromised. As we have seen, the more species present in a system, the more stable it is and better able to withstand perturbations in the populations and number of species present. When the number of species becomes very small, a small event can have a very large outcome. Think in terms of a circle of four species, each one dependent on the previous species in the circle. While it is in balance all will go well, but if one of the species is removed or much reduced in numbers, the three other species will have lost either their direct or indirect support and consequently will themselves be in danger of disappearing.

Dependencies such as these are more often found in highly specialised species, such as cuckoo bumblebees that rely on another species for nesting sites. An example of this, though only one of many, is the vestal cuckoo bumblebee (*Bombus vestalis*), which is widespread throughout the UK. Like all the cuckoo bumblebees, this species takes over the nest of other bumblebees in which to rear their young. In the case of the vestal cuckoo, the target species is the buff-tailed bumblebee (*Bombus terrestris*), another widespread and relatively common species. The females of the vestal cuckoo can be found as early as March searching out host nesting sites. This relationship is a relatively stable one because both species are widespread and common. In fact, the buff-tailed is in an unusual position for a bumblebee because it is a very important pollinator of glasshouse crops. This value to the glasshouse crop industry has resulted in it being bred in captivity specifically to act as a primary pollinator. Colonies of buff-tailed can be quite large with 300 or so individuals and while variation in wild populations is very limited, captive bred colonies have a greater variation in appearance. Here we have two different species of bumblebee that both forage for nectar, but one is independent (buff-tailed) and the other dependent (vestal cuckoo). This is not an unusual situation among bumblebees and many other species of insect as well. We have said that one species is dependent upon the other, but this is a very simple way of looking at the situation.

What we have seen with the relationship between buff-tailed and vestal cuckoo bumblebees is a story that becomes more convoluted and complex the deeper that it is looked at. Both of these species forage for nectar on flowering plants, Buff-taileds will also collect pollen for the nest, but vestal cuckoos do not. This does not mean that one is a better pollinator than the other as this is a process that takes place as an accidental part of the feeding process. Like bumblebees, many insects are generalist feeders, visiting a lot of different species of flowers and being dusted with, and spreading, pollen as they go. However, what makes bumblebees do a good and reliable job of it is that, during any particular period, they visit just one or two species, usually a major and a minor. In the right area, these flowers will sometimes be wild thyme, which will then set seed to feed *Myrmica sabuleti*, the ant that looks after the large blue butterfly that also feeds on wild thyme in its early stages. So although many of these species have no direct contact with each other and would not figure in an energy or nutrient flow diagram of an ecosystem, their interactions are an important part of a healthy meadow. It is for this reason that it is so often said that the more species there are the more stable an ecosystem is. All parts are connected together in some way, even if we cannot clearly quantify exactly what the relationship is. This apparent importance without direct interaction is sometimes referred to as amensalism and can be seen in cases where grasshoppers can interrupt feeding in caterpillars of butterfly species if they are present in large numbers by causing a 'predator freeze' response in the caterpillars. This has been shown to affect growth rates and survival in some species by constantly interrupting the otherwise continuous feeding that caterpillars engage in.

In this complicated, but essentially robust and stable, biological system, introducing alien species can have an upsetting effect. Sometimes species have been here for so long that they are regarded as part of the scenery, an integral part of the ecosystem. One such species is the rabbit (*Oryctolagus cuniculus*) (Figure 8.6). Originally brought to Britain by the Romans, it seems that these would have been kept as pets in cages so they were unable to establish themselves in the wild. There may have been other reasons for this lack of establishment in the wild, but we can only surmise what these were. At the time of the Roman occupation, there were three species widely found in Great Britain that would have enjoyed a meal of rabbit. These lost species are wolf, cat and eagle. The grey wolf (*Canis lupus*) became extinct in England about 1500, but lingered on in small numbers in Scotland for another 250 years. Our native wildcat (*Felis silvestris*) disappeared from southern England in about 1750 and northern England and Wales by 1890. In Scotland, where it still survives, it is well known as an eater of rabbits. The same is true of the third large predator, the golden eagle (*Aquila chrysaetos*), which, although lost from England and Wales around 1850, has survived in Scotland.

Figure 8.6. *Rabbits photographed in our meadow using a motion-sensitive camera.*

The major introduction of the rabbit that helped change our landscape took place when the Normans invaded in the eleventh century. They brought rabbits to the UK for both food and fur, and originally introduced them onto islands off the south coast of England. By the thirteenth century they had been moved to the mainland, where they became established as a feral species. With the passing centuries, the presence of rabbits in the countryside has become accepted and expected. However, they do affect the ecology of communities where they live. For example, they can provide the grazing that is key to the large blue and *Myrmica sabuleti*. They make a difference to life in our large meadow by digging and the production of scrapes (Figure 8.7). The scrapes open the soil to germination of seeds and the digging of holes can be used by other species. One of the frequent users of abandoned rabbit and vole holes are wasps and we usually have three of their nests in the meadow, always associated with mammal digging. There is a secondary link here, as well, because the wasps can become food for badgers (*Meles meles*), as was demonstrated one day in the large meadow (Figures 8.8 and 8.9).

Besides the rabbit, we have another alien mammal species that uses the large meadow, muntjac (*Muntiacus reevesi*) (Figure 8.10). It likes to shelter in our thicket of bramble (*Rubus fruticosus* agg.) and gorse (*Ulex europaeus*). The muntjac was brought to the UK in the first half of the nineteenth century for London Zoo and later the deer

Figure 8.7. *A scrape created in the large meadow by male rabbits. These scrapes give space and time for plants to germinate without pressure from grass.*

Figure 8.8. *A badger dug up this wasp nest in the large meadow. The wasps are now trying to repair it, but rain finished the job that the badger started.*

Figure 8.9. *A night vision photograph of a badger in transit across our meadow boundary. Blurring is an artefact of the slow shutter speed.*

Figure 8.10. *Reeves's muntjac captured on film in the large meadow.*

park at Woburn. By 1900 they had escaped, or were deliberately released, and were known to be breeding in the wild, and now they have spread to become widespread in England and Wales and are moving north towards Scotland. Both rabbit and muntjac are grazers introduced by man, but muntjac is considered to be detrimental because it can badly affect woodland regeneration. It is perceived as an alien invader, while the rabbit tends to be thought of as a 'natural' part of the environment. There are a few reasons for this. The rabbit has been here for almost 800 years, sufficient time to become an integral part of the ecosystem, which has rebalanced to accommodate it with several natural predators – fox (*Vulpes vulpes*), badger, weasel (*Mustela nivalis*), stoat (*Mustela erminea*) – and there is evidence that it was part of the UK's fauna in the interglacial period, so it is possible that but for the last Ice Age it would be a native species anyway. Conversely, the muntjac is, in ecological terms, a recent arrival, it has no natural predators and it was never native here nor would it ever be likely to arrive naturally given that it is native to south-east China. Perhaps muntjac should not be picked out in this, as of the six deer species naturalised in the UK, only two, red and roe, are truly indigenous.

The problem with alien species is that they have the potential to wreak havoc with existing ecosystems because the complex interactions with other species that keep them in check where they are native are not part of the ecosystem they have been introduced into. We have many examples of this in Britain: Himalayan balsam (*Impatiens glandulifera*) and rhododendron (*Rhododendron ponticum*) in the plant world, *Ophiostoma novo-ulmi* and *Ophiostoma ulmi*, causing Dutch elm disease, and *Hymenoscyphus fraxineus*, causing ash dieback, among the fungi, and Asian hornet (*Vespa velutina*) and American mink (*Neovison vison*) among animal introductions. Given enough time, and this probably means centuries, aliens can settle into an ecosystem and can become an important part of it; just two examples from Britain are rabbits and sycamore (*Acer pseudoplatanus*).

A major aspect of meadow ecology, in fact ecology everywhere, that is easily overlooked is that of the soil itself. There is as much, perhaps more, going on underground as above ground. Beyond the obvious activity within the soil of earthworms and all the other invertebrates, from burrowing dung beetles to building ants, a major part of the soil is made up of bacteria and fungi. Soil fertility has three broad components: physical, chemical and biological. The physical component is all about the texture of the soil and its water-holding capacity, all the purely mechanical aspects of the soil. In contrast, the chemical component is all about the acidity of the soil and the solubility of nutrients held in it. The last part, biological fertility, is what is living in the soil, and more specifically the micro-organisms that are present. Although there are pathogenic micro-organisms found in soil, most of those normally present are doing a good job in maintaining the health and fertility of our meadows.

The two groups of micro-organisms of greatest significance in soil are bacteria and fungi. A large proportion of both of these groups are decomposers, consuming complex biological material and making simpler chemical compounds available for use by other organisms, most often plants. This is an especially valuable function with regards to old plant material as it is only micro-organisms that have an active ability to digest cellulose from plant cell walls and lignin from wood. Although many animals eat this material, it is only through the micro-organisms in their gut that the full value of the nutrient content is released. Huge quantities of these two groups of organisms grow in our soils. It is said that fertile soil contains about 1 tonne of bacteria per acre of land, and, although this is hard to verify, it is easily shown that in most soils 75% of micro-organisms are found in the top 5cm.

As well as the decomposers, another significant clade of micro-organisms are mutualists. In this category are the mycorrhizal fungi, which have a very close relationship with green plants and a major ability to render phosphorous soluble so that it can be readily absorbed by plants. There are two broad groups of mutualists, ectomycorrhizae and endomycorrhizae. The ectomycorrhizae are root surface colonisers and are primarily associated with trees. In a meadow it is the endomycorrhizae that are of greater significance as these are species that infiltrate the roots of plants and grow within plant cells. It is now thought that almost all meadow plants can form mycorrhizal associations, but there is one group of plants for whom these invasive fungi are essential – orchids. Orchid seed is minute, with no nutrients stored within, so to germinate the seed has to be infiltrated by an appropriate fungus, which supplies essential material to the seed to get it started. Without the fungal associate it cannot germinate and for many species this is a lifelong association. This is described in more detail in Chapter 5.

Soil bacteria produce polysaccharides and mucilage, which binds soil particles together. Fungi do much the same thing, but by growing as filaments they tend to produce binding nets in among the soil particles as well. It is this that allows soil to stick together when gently squeezed in the hand, although this is not to be mistaken for the colloidal processes found in clay. When soil is very dry it does not stick to itself simply because the lack of water is affecting the bacteria and fungi.

An aspect of soil bacteria activity that is of great importance in meadows is nitrogen fixation. In soils this is carried out by species of *Nitrobacter* and *Nitrosomonas*. This same process is carried out in root nodules by species of *Rhizobia*. These are species that have a close association with legumes. Although *Rhizobia* can live as a free-living species, it can only express its genes for nitrogen fixation when it is living with a host species in nodules on the roots. Among the species commonly found in meadows, it is the clovers and vetches that carry *Rhizobia*, although not on the scale of commercial legumes like peas and beans.

From the soil, nutrients move through the various organisms that are found in the meadow, usually starting with bacteria or fungi, into plants and then the herbivorous animals and then their predators and so on. Each time the process takes a step forward, some waste material is returned to the soil and recycled. At each stage of this the useable energy decreases, as would be expected from the Second Law of Thermodynamics, such that in a closed system the amount of useable energy will always decline. However, the meadow is not a closed system; it gains regular and continuous amounts of energy from the sun, which is used in photosynthesis to produce chemical complexity and order in the form of growth and development in the flowering plants. It is the green plants that are the primary producers of organic matter as they are the only organisms present that capture energy, in the form of sunlight. Photosynthesis is a fundamental process that takes carbon dioxide and water to create sugars. This is an energy-consuming process and the plants utilise the energy of sunlight to carry out the manufacture. As a process, photosynthesis is only about 26% efficient, so not all the energy absorbed is used. Not only that, but only about 34% of the light falling on a leaf is absorbed and used. This latter point is self-evident because plants are green, so green light is reflected or transmitted and not absorbed by the plant. Other wavelengths of light are utilised at different rates, hence the apparently low efficiency rate.

As plants use energy for respiration and growth, the efficiency of photosynthesis as a process is of less significance in the ecology of a meadow than the amount of stored energy the plant creates. This figure is about 1% of the absorbed energy becoming available to be used by other plants and animals as the plants are eaten or collapse and decay. Another way of looking at this is slightly away from a meadow, but does give an idea of the scale of photosynthesis as the primary producer. Fast-growing willow varieties can sequester 7.3 tonnes of carbon per year per hectare, or if you prefer, 26.8 tonnes of carbon dioxide per year per hectare removed from the atmosphere. Grassland carbon sequestration tends to be less per hectare, but even so it is significant on an annual basis. If the cut grass is stored it will keep the sequestered carbon tied up until it is returned either to the ground by being ploughed in, or the atmosphere by being burnt or digested by a grazer.

The flow of energy within a meadow can be a useful way of expressing movement of nutrients, but it is a very difficult process to measure. When it has been successful it results in a scheme that almost looks as though the energy itself is an organism within the ecosystem. This way of expressing the interactions within a meadow can tell us a great deal about the ecosystem, but not everything. Energy flow may just not be applicable to the strange and complicated ways that all the different species interact, without one eating the other, or provide any direct and easily explained reason for their being neighbours. In a way, when I sit in the meadow and grasshoppers land on me as a perch I become part of the ecology, an amensalist, a species without direct interaction with other species. This is the best way of being in a meadow; not interacting, just looking and enjoying.

CHAPTER 9

The future

We have changed. We mostly live in cities. If we go to the countryside at all it is at weekends or on holiday. Two hundred and fifty years ago, before the industrial revolution, 80% of the population worked on the land as farmers, farm workers, or in supporting occupations such as millers, blacksmiths and farriers. Most people lived in small villages of one or two hundred souls. Villages were quite closely spaced. People walked to work and meadows were commonplace. Farms were small and every one of them would have hay meadows, or if they did not, they would have local access to hay from a nearby farm. Hay from the meadows was essential to keep stock and the working horses alive over the winter; without it they would starve. So at that time most of the population saw meadows every day and got to revel in their glory every summer, even if they did not realise the benefit of having them. Meadows were as central to people's lives as food, the church and the pub. This was how it had been for generations, with a farming year that had not changed for 2,000 years or more.

This all began to change, gradually at first, with the introduction of mechanisation and better transport – canals and railways – and importing concentrated fertiliser in the form of guano. The changes were slow, until the biggest change came seventy years ago with the full onslaught of the green revolution – complete mechanisation, artificial fertilisers and chemical agents such as herbicides, pesticides and fungicides. Along with this came improved varieties of grass and seed cleaning. Horses were no longer needed and stock could be overwintered on silage. Old meadows once improved could yield three or four cuts of grass for silage every year. Traditional meadows became an anachronism and were simply swept away. The large numbers of farm workers were not needed either and we moved from the countryside to the cities.

Today in Britain four-fifths of us live in urban areas, two thirds in cities, one fifth in rural areas and only 1.2% of the population actually work on the land. We have lost 97% of the traditional meadows that existed in the 1930s, something like 3 million hectares have gone, and probably close to 99% of them since their heyday before the industrial revolution. It is reckoned that there are only 15,000 hectares of good-quality grassland still in existence. That is about the same as the area of Glasgow and only four-fifths of the area we allocate to car parks. And this 15,000 hectares includes unimproved pasture as well as meadow and most of it is in tiny, and therefore, vulnerable fragments. The true area of high-quality traditional meadow still existing must be much smaller. The upshot is that the vast majority of us can no longer see meadows on our doorstep; most likely we will have to travel many miles to catch a glimpse of one.

Our predecessors knew very well the importance of hay but they almost certainly did not appreciate the other benefits meadows brought them. That they feed our souls and grow pollinators for our crops would have been taken for granted, because this was as it had always been. They had no experience of not having meadows and therefore of not having these two benefits. That meadows store carbon, delay water run-off and boost diversity would have been completely beyond our predecessors' ken. These things were simply not important then; they did not have a climate crisis and nature was not in meltdown. Today though, all of these benefits are invaluable and mean that meadows should be just as important to us as they were for our forebears.

If there is one thing the isolation of the Covid-19 pandemic that started in 2020 has shown us, it is that nature brings us comfort and eases our mental stresses. It is a food for the soul. Meadows full of flowers are joyful. A simple local pasture full of thigh-high buttercups was a huge magnet during lockdown. People smiled and the children and dogs dashed about. Children especially are enthralled by meadows. There is always something for them to discover and they are particularly fascinated by the numerous insects that are always plentiful in flower meadows.

Many of these insects are the ones that will have been pollinating our crops in gardens, allotments or the surrounding fields, or will be going on to pollinate them. It has been estimated that as many as 75% of all crops around the world depend on pollination and in 2005 alone insect-pollinated crops were reckoned to be worth £127 billion. Needless to say that lots of insects and spiders means lots of food for birds.

Underground, when the dark laboratory that we do not fully understand is functioning properly, fungi, bacteria and plants have the ability to interact, helping to lock up carbon. As Ian Dunn from the charity Plantlife put it succinctly 'up to 30% of the world's carbon is stored in grassland carbon sinks – meaning grasslands are every bit as important as forests and other ecosystems in the fight against greenhouse gases'. This diversity above and below ground is key to the web of life. It keeps things nice and stable. Pests and diseases are controlled without resorting to chemicals. We unbalance this at our peril.

Modern 'improved' meadows may be more productive than the flower-rich traditional meadow in terms of the weight of fodder harvested from them, but when it comes to these other services they do not compare. The pure grass mixtures that are sown mean there are no flowers, no pollinators, no birds, no diversity, no joy. The continual working, ploughing, relaying and applying of artificial dressings, compacts and damages the soil, depletes the soil fauna and flora, and disrupts the dark laboratory, meaning less carbon is captured and poorer water storage. The hugely reduced above- and below-ground diversity makes the system unstable and the modern meadow requires ever more artificial input to maintain it.

Thus it seems only good sense to make more room for traditional-style flower meadows in the countryside and also in urban areas. A meadows movement has been under way for some time now and there is some optimism for the future.

Plantlife, the charitable organisation championing our native flora, as well as having twenty or so meadow reserves of its own, has been at the forefront of many of the initiatives looking to save those fragments of traditional meadow still existing and to create new ones. Perhaps the biggest of these initiatives was prompted by HRH The Prince of Wales, who in 2012 called for the creation of a new wild flower meadow in every county to celebrate the anniversary of the Coronation. Plantlife in partnership with the Wildlife Trusts and the Rare Breeds Survival Trust took up this challenge. They have identified the best example of a traditional meadow still existing in each county and nominated it as the county's Coronation Meadow. The plan is to create new meadows, called Recipient Meadows, on land specially selected as suitable in every county from seed donated by the county's Coronation Meadow. In this way it is hoped to maintain the local character in the new meadows. So far some ninety new meadows have been created. The Coronation Meadows Project also records what it calls Peoples Meadows. These are sites nominated by the public as great places to see meadow flowers.

In 2014 Plantlife led another countrywide initiative, called Save Our Magnificent Meadows, to restore 6,000 hectares of degraded wildflower meadow and activities to give people the chance to celebrate meadows. The project, which was funded by the Heritage Lottery and brought together eleven conservation organisations, ended in 2017, but National Meadows Day is still celebrated in July every year, the website continues to provide useful advice and guidance, and the partners can be contacted to discover opportunities to join in meadow conservation.

The county Wildlife Trusts have for many years brought fine examples of traditional meadows under their wing when they have become available and have worked hard to replicate the management required to keep them in good condition. There are not many of these sites though and they are often very small. They list just over forty of their reserves as meadow, although some are really pasture. They also take part in local initiatives. For example, Pollinating Cheshire aims to restore or create 100 hectares of meadow over a ten-year period.

As its name suggests, the Flood Plain Meadows Partnership is a partnership of nine environmental organisations, including Wildlife Trusts, Natural England, the RSPB and the National Trust, working to identify, protect and restore the special meadows that develop on flood plains in England and Wales. They have recorded just over 500 flood plain meadows in their database, which sounds like a lot but many are tiny fragments of land and their quality is not always known. The total area remaining is estimated at less than 1,500 hectares. Flood plain meadows were the richest, most productive meadows and some of the remaining fragments are ancient indeed, with archaeological evidence stretching back to the Bronze Age for the Oxford meadows and to Roman times for meadows associated with the River Ouse.

The RSPB and National Trust have both created flower meadows on their land and work to manage much of their estate in a more traditional way by conservation grazing with cattle and ponies. They also have working model farms with which they are trying to persuade more of the farming community to run their farms in a more nature-friendly way. At Hope Farm outside Cambridge the RSPB has demonstrated that it can still maintain its profits when it has turned over 15% of its marginal land for conservation. This includes planting up seed-rich field margins, which can be meadow-like so long as they are permanent and the plants chosen are native wildflowers.

It is also true that some farmers have already taken the difficult path and turned their backs on modern intensive farming practices, as is wonderfully described by James Rebanks in his book *English Pastoral*. Finally, there are the private individuals who are restoring or creating field-sized meadows much as we have been describing for the large meadow. In a recent visit to Devon I came across two of these, one forming the centre of a large campsite field. Here the meadow is simply an improved pasture that is left unmown during the summer, so the flowers will be mostly the ubiquitous buttercups and red and white clover, but still a joy to the campers who can wander the paths cut through it. The other is a section of a tea plantation that was improved pasture and has been returned to traditional hay meadow management with reintroduction of native wildflowers. There must be many more examples like this across the country.

There are ambitious plans, too. Plantlife is calling for restoration of 120,000 hectares of wildflower meadow by 2043 and the UK government has pledged to protect 30% of our land for nature by 2030 by signing up to the UN's Leaders Pledge for Nature, and surely some of this must be wildflower meadow.

This is all tremendous and very encouraging but let us not over-egg progress to give the impression that everything is now sorted. Many of the meadows included in the initiatives are double, perhaps even triple counted. Augill Meadow, for example, is listed as both a Plantlife reserve and a Cumbria Wildlife Trust reserve, and Seaton Meadows in Rutland is both a Plantlife reserve and a Coronation Meadow. Pledges, plans and targets, especially those made by a government for a future beyond their term of office, do not always work out. The UK government's pledge to protect 30% of our land for nature may be an empty promise anyway since they already claim 28% is protected by virtue of being included in National Parks and Areas of Outstanding Natural Beauty, but, in reality, these offer almost no protection. A more considered survey by the RSPB says that right now only 5% is effectively protected. We are probably still losing some old meadows for a variety of reasons. The owner may decide to use the land for some other purpose or simply stops managing it in a meadow-centric way; since the remaining meadows are usually on less productive land or land that is awkward to manage, they are often taken for development in preference to 'good' agricultural land; or they may be on a path of gradual decline anyway because their special plants, which are now living in sub-optimal conditions surrounded by intensively managed farmland, are not producing enough seed to maintain themselves.

We also feel a certain amount of nervousness that the meadows movement may be losing impetus with the focus of conservationists and environmentalists turning to more recent imperatives. The danger can be seen in the rush to plant trees that resulted in more than one meadow being over-planted. Thankfully the trees were quickly removed when the problem was highlighted and, in fact, it helped to drive an initiative to use the huge Botanical Society of Britain and Ireland's plant distribution database to map hot areas and make this information more readily available to planners. Likewise, re-wilding could be a threat. Since meadows are arguably the zenith of semi-natural vegetation, relying absolutely on management by man, they are simultaneously the antithesis of re-wilding. It would be foolish indeed to include any ancient meadows in a re-wilding scheme with the hope that they would survive due to natural processes alone. Then there are green energy schemes that consume agricultural land. Wind and solar panel farms physically cover land; grass mills that turn grass into gas in a carbon neutral way, but require 0.75 acres per home and manage grassland too intensively for flower meadows to survive, could consume vast areas of grassland. Of course, we encourage all of these environmental schemes but please not at the expense of meadows, either by physically destroying them or diverting resources. Finally, the National Trust, partner in some of the initiatives described above, is considering selling Clayton Meadows in Studland for development. This property was gifted to them specifically to conserve the meadows.

Sadly, even multiple conservation designations – Sites of Special Scientific Interest and such like – do not always seem to be able to stop development. The losing battle between HS2 and ancient woodland is a good example of this. There can be no mitigation for the loss of ancient woodland unless one accepts the argument that replacement plantings will one day, 500 years or so hence, do the job. Ancient meadows are analogous, except in their case we probably only have to wait decades. The other mitigation sometimes proposed for meadows is to move them, but this is more often than not unsuccessful in the long term because it is almost impossible to replicate the conditions of the old site – hydrology, micro-climate, sub-soil, etc – at the new location. In the future it would be wonderful to have the primacy of designated sites fully instituted. After all, they make up such a tiny proportion of the countryside.

One way or another we have to pay for all of this if we want to maintain the countryside for our collective benefit. How we do it is open to question but a sensible approach might be to start paying a realistic price for food, but only if the government can somehow ensure that the extra money goes to the people who look after the land and that the people who look after the land do it in a nature-friendly way. The problem is the pressure from big agriculture, which tends to push back against anything that might threaten the status quo and threaten their profits. This can only really be overcome by equal lobbying and pressure on the side of nature, which means mobilising people. Unfortunately, at the moment for a majority of the population nature is a bit 'so what?' Our connection to nature and the countryside has gradually eroded over the years and, until the pandemic, many had forgotten the pleasure we humans get from contact with nature and had not understood how good it is for our well-being.

For meadows the really important thing is to get people into them and to celebrate and appreciate their intrinsic delight. If we want to save them we need as much public support as we can muster. One way of doing this would be to make better use of the information we already have access to and make a unified inventory. I find it time consuming and quite hard work to navigate all of the various websites to find the local meadows open to the public when I am going to a new part of the country, and I am both a meadow enthusiast and an IT expert. The Wildlife Trusts' website cluster is particularly clunky. There should be a much easier route for people to discover where their local meadows are and what they are likely to see at the time of looking. If the information is not easily accessible the casual browser will pretty quickly give up.

Meadows in gardens and parks are important in bringing people to appreciate meadows as well, since most of us want to get our contact with nature on our doorstep just like our forebears. If we have to travel miles we probably will not bother unless there is some other interest as well. The garden is literally on our doorstep. We hope that books like this one will encourage more people to turn over a part of their garden to meadow, and we applaud the TV and radio gardening programmes and magazines, such as the RSPB's *Nature's Home*, that occasionally promote the garden meadow. Parks and other green spaces, like road verges, under council control are the closest piece of nature for many people and many of these are being turned into meadow-like spaces by the simple measure of carefully timing a reduced number of mowings. Plantlife's road verge campaign is playing a great part in this. Gardens and parks cover a huge area of the country as well. Gardens alone cover 5%. They are also the perfect habitat for encouraging diversity, which reaches its height where there are lots of features, like hedgerows, trees, ponds and so on, in close proximity.

One last thing. Those old pastoral landscapes are just as much part of our cultural heritage as the old buildings that were erected by the farming community or with the profits from farming – the barns, churches, water mills and stately homes – that we spend so much money and time on to conserve. Why aren't we making the same effort to save those precious parcels of landscape that still exist?

It is difficult to overplay the pleasure and interest our two meadows have given us. There is so much contentment wandering through or sitting in the meadow in its summer glory: bees busying themselves, hoverflies dancing in the air, butterflies drifting on the breeze that sweeps across the elegant grasses and bright flowers. Even the work of mowing reconnects us with some distant sense of fulfilment. And so for us, trying to conserve them is not some exercise in futility, some misplaced nostalgia, some random sticking of a pin in earth's history to get back to what it was, but a place to recapture what for 2,000 years was in our DNA, a chance to regain diversity, to help fight the scourge of global warming, to boost well-being, to bring joy.

> A clouded sky dulls the herbage, a cloudless heaven brightens it, so that the grass almost reflects the firmament like water. At sunset the rosy rays bring out every tint of red or purple. At noonday, watch as alternate shadow and sunshine come one after the other as the clouds are wafted over. By moonlight perhaps the white ox-eyed daisies show the most. But never will you find the mowing grass in the same field looking twice alike.
>
> *Nature Near London*, Richard Jefferies

> When daisies pied, and violets blue,
> And lady-smocks all silver-white,
> And cuckoo-buds of yellow hue
> Do paint the meadows with delight.
>
> Song in *Love's Labours Lost*, William Shakespeare

References and Further Reading

General

Darwin, C. (1881) *The formation of vegetable mould, through the action of worms, with observations on their habits.* John Murray, London.

Eatherley, D. (2019) *Invasive Aliens.* William Collins, London.

Goulson, D. (2014) *A Buzz in the Meadow.* Vintage Books, London.

Jefferies, R. (1879) *The Amateur Poacher.* Smith Elder and Co., London. Many modern reprints are available.

Jefferies, R. (1883) *Nature Near London.* Chatto and Windus, London. Many modern reprints are available.

Leopold, A. (1949) *A Sand County Almanac and Sketches Here and There.* Oxford University Press, New York.

Lewis-Stempel, J. (2014) *Meadowland.* Black Swan, London.

Macdonald, B. (2019) *Rebirding.* Pelagic Publishing, Exeter.

Percival, M. (1950). Pollen Presentation and Collection. *New Phytologist* 49: 40–63

Peterken, G. (2013). *Meadows.* British Wildlife Publishing, Gillingham.

Rackham, O. (2000) *The History of the Countryside.* Phoenix Publishing, London.

Rebanks, J. (2021) *English Pastoral: An Inheritance.* Penguin, London.

Tree, I. (2018) *Wilding.* Picador, London.

Wright, J. (2017) *A Natural History of the Hedgerow.* Profile Books, London.

Identification guides

There are very many field guides to help in identifying all of the various plants and animals that may appear in the meadow. These are the ones that we use regularly.

Bang, P. and Dahlstrom, P. (2001) *Animal Tracks and Signs.* Oxford University Press, Oxford.

Barnard, P. (2011) *The Royal Entomological Society Book of British Insects.* Wiley-Blackwell, West Sussex.

Blamey, M., Fitter, R. and Fitter, A. (2003) *Wild Flowers of Britain and Ireland.* Domino Books Ltd, Jersey

Carter, D. (1982) *Butterflies and Moths in Britain and Europe.* Pan Books, London.

Clapham, A. R., Tutin, T. G. and Warburg, E. F. (1962) *Flora Of The British Isles.* Cambridge University Press, Cambridge.

Evans, M. and Edmondson, R. (2007) *A photographic Guide to the Grasshoppers and Crickets of Britain and Ireland.* WILDGuides Publishing.

Falk, S. and Lewington, R. (2016) *Field Guide to the Bees of Great Britain and Ireland.* Bloomsbury, London.

Higgins, L. and Riley, N. (1980) *A Field Guide to the Butterflies of Britain and Europe.* Collins, London.

Lowen, J. (2021) *British Moths.* Bloomsbury, London.

Roberts, M. (1995) *Field Guide to Spiders of Britain and Northern Europe.* Harper Collins, Publishers, London.

Rose, F. (1989) *Grasses, Sedges, Rushes and Ferns of the British Isles and North-western Europe.* Penguin, London.

Stace, C. (2019) *New Flora of the British Isles.* Fourth Edition. C&M Floristics, Suffolk (The plant scientific names used in this book are those from 'Stace 4'.)

Sterry, P. (2006) *Collins Complete Guide to British Wild Flowers.* Harper Collins, London.

Sterry, P. (2009) *Collins Complete Guide to British Mushrooms and Toadstools.* Harper Collins, London.

Townsend, M. and Waring, P. (2007) *Concise Guide to the Moths of Great Britain and Ireland.* British Wildlife Publishing, Dorset.

Yeo, P. and Corbet, S. (2015) *Solitary Wasps.* Naturalists' Handbook 3. Pelagic Publishing, Exeter.

Resources

This list of resources is not exhaustive and there are certainly others that might better suit your needs. It is a list of those resources that we have found useful and would recommend.

Equipment

Scythes and hay rakes

Simon Fairlie (Scythes), Monkton Wyld Court, Charmouth, Dorset, DT6 6DQ, www.thescytheshop.co.uk

Scythe Cymru Dyfed, Permaculture Farm Trust, Carmarthenshire, SA44 5HG, www.scythecymru.co.uk

The Natural Gardener, Knowbury, Shropshire, SY8 3JP, www.thenaturalgardener.co.uk

Mechanical cutters

Mow Direct, Sandy, Bedfordshire, SG19 1SB, www.mowdirect.co.uk

Greenstripe Garden Machinery, Market Rasen, Lincs, LN8 3LY, www.greenstripe.net

Seeds

Emorsgate Seeds, Limes Farm, Tilney All Saints, King's Lynn, Norfolk, PE34 4RT, www.wildseed.co.uk

Naturescape Wildflowers, Maple Farm, Langar, Nottinghamshire, NG13 9HP, www.naturescape.co.uk

Wild Flower Lawns and Meadows, Downsview Farm, Horam, East Sussex, TN21 9HJ, www.wildflowerlawnsandmeadows.com

Yellow Flag Wildflowers, 8 Plock Court, Longford, Gloucester, GL2 9DW, www.wildflowersuk.com

Collection and observation
Sweep nets
nhbs Ltd, Totnes, Devon, TQ9 5LE,
www.nhbs.com
Motion-sensitive trap cameras
Gardenature Limited, Clacton on Sea, Essex, CO15 4TL,
www.gardenature.co.uk

Online Help

Ellenberg Indicator Values
http://nora.nerc.ac.uk/id/eprint/6411/1/ECOFACT2a.pdf

Making meadows
Floodplain Meadows Partnership, Floodplain Meadows – Beauty and Utility. A Technical Handbook, www.floodplainmeadows.org.uk/sites/www.floodplainmeadows.org.uk/files/Floodplain%20Meadows%20-%20Beauty%20and%20Utility%20A%20Technical%20Handbook.pdf
Magnificent Meadows,
www.magnificentmeadows.org.uk/advice-guidance
Plant distribution maps
BSBI,
https://bsbi.org/maps

Societies

Botanical Society of Britain and Ireland, 28 Chipchase Grove, Durham, DH1 3FA, www.bsbi.org
Buglife, G.06, Allia Future Business Centre, London Road, Peterborough, PE2 8AN, www.buglife.org.uk
Plantlife, Brewery House, 36 Milford Street, Salisbury, Wiltshire, SP12 2AP, www.plantlife.org.uk
Royal Society for the Protection of Birds (RSPB). The Lodge, Potton Road, Sandy, SG19 2DL, www.rspb.org.uk

Index

Page numbers in *italics* refer to illustrations

I

J

K

L

O

P

Q

R